SWING PERFECT

To a perfect swinger

Bob

SWING PERFECT

Neil Tappin

THE EASY WAY TO AN IMMACULATE SWING

hamlyn

First published in Great Britain in 2007 by
Hamlyn, a division of Octopus Publishing Group Ltd
2–4 Heron Quays, London E14 4JP

Distributed in the United States and Canada by
Sterling Publishing Co., Inc.
387 Park Avenue South, New York, NY 10016-8810

ISBN-13: 978-0-600-61553-8
ISBN-10: 0-600-61553-7

A CIP catalogue record for this book is available from the British Library

Printed and bound in China

10 9 8 7 6 5 4 3 2 1

Note: The text has been written from the point of view of teaching a
right-handed player. For left-handed players, reverse the advice given
to read 'left' for 'right' and vice-versa.

Photography shot at West Kent Golf Club, Kent, England

CONTENTS

INTRODUCTION

Ever since the game that we recognize today was first played on the windswept Scottish coastline, golfers have striven to master the perfect swing. Such a movement combines power with poise while sending the ball on a towering flight, homing in on its target with pinpoint accuracy. The sight of just one of these great shots and the feelings that a smooth but dynamic swing evoke will leave you hooked, desperate to relive this moment of glory time and again.

But golf's great attraction is also its inevitable frustration. One wrong move can cause a duff strike or wayward shot that has you scratching your head, desperately searching for answers. The good news is that as golf has become ever more popular over the last decade, so the tuition available has vastly improved, arming players with all the knowledge required to perform to their best ability.

Golfers are better placed now than ever before to understand how the key movements in the swing can affect the resulting shot. At the heart of consistently clean and accurate ball striking is the address position, that is the position of your body just before you start the swing. Cementing good fundamentals of stance, grip and posture will trigger a chain reaction of positive movements that makes a good shot the most likely outcome.

Once you have mastered the essential set-up position and the basic swing mechanics, you will be able to experiment with your ball flight in a bid to take your game to the next level. Using sidespin to shape your shots through the air will help you cope with the specific challenges of any course, from manicured inland to blustery links. If you can also manipulate the trajectory of your shots, then tough weather conditions should not prevent you from recording an impressive score.

Few sports place a player's mental strength under the microscope quite as much as golf. Nervous tension will build up – threatening to hamper the fluidity of your swing – when you are standing on the first tee of a strokeplay competition, in which the player who takes the lowest number of shots to complete the round will top the leaderboard, or when you are looking to finish off a good round. Coping with this pressure is an important skill that will help you maintain a high level of performance just as you need it the most. Blocking out negative thoughts and preventing self-doubt from wrecking a usually solid swing is what separates the very best golfers from the rest.

Whether you are just starting out or you are striving to elevate your game to the next level, *Swing Perfect* will guide you through all you need to know – from buying the right set of clubs and setting sound fundamentals to manipulating your ball flight and coping with pressure. The instruction that follows has been broken down into concise, easy to understand sections, with step-by-step guides and effective drills designed to improve your performance. So whether you read this book straight through from start to finish or use it as a handy reference, you should find all its tips and advice provide an invaluable aid in your pursuit to swing perfect.

EQUIPMENT

Before you set about building a successful swing, you need to invest in a set of clubs. But with so many different makes and models on the market, finding something to suit your eye at the right price can seem daunting. This chapter guides you through what is available and for what standard of golfer it is suitable, so that you can find a formula that meets your needs.

Drivers
The majority of modern drivers fall into one of three categories: drivers with titanium heads; those with composite heads; and those with heads that contain adjustable weights.

Titanium heads
The most common of these are drivers with titanium heads. These are made of strong, durable but light metal, which has enabled manufacturers to move weight deeper and lower in the clubhead. The loud 'ping' that can be heard at impact from such titanium heads is said to resonate confidence through your game.

Composite heads
By adding extra light graphite to the crown of a titanium-headed driver manufacturers can force the centre of gravity lower in the head. The slightly muted impact sound of this driver type has, in the past, put off some golfers (but manufacturers are working on this).

(top) Various titanium and composite driver heads.

(above) With movable weights in the head, players should be able to find their ideal trajectory and shape.

Head with adjustable weights
The latest type of drivers has movable weights in the head. The idea here is that you can set up the club to help you find the perfect shape of shot, if for example you are playing a course that requires plenty of right-to-left, drawing tee shots. It is important to know that changing the weights to correct a destructive flight can do more harm than good.

Type of driver	Use for	Ideal for
Titanium head	increasing the ball's trajectory for longer carries	inconsistent ball strikers looking for the confidence of a larger sweet spot
Composite head	increasing launch angle; lowering spin rate	golfers who struggle to get the ball airborne easily and those after a straighter flight
Heads with adjustable weights	more flexibility to alter the ball flight	golfers looking to manipulate the trajectory and shape of their drives

Fairway woods

When selecting fairway woods you have three similar choices over the type of head to go for.

Titanium fairway woods tend to have large heads that inspire confidence in a sweet strike when looking down at address.

Steel, however, still remains the most popular choice when it comes to fairway woods. They tend to be slightly more compact and playable than titanium versions and are also a little less pricey. Their superior playability means that golfers can manipulate the flight of the ball, and it allows better players to assume more control over the shot they are playing.

A third head option to consider is composite heads. These are a sort of halfway house between steel and titanium, and they offer players many benefits of both.

Size matters

One of your toughest decisions when picking a driver or fairway wood is over the size of the head. The basic principle is that bigger heads with larger faces offer generous sweet spots, thus increasing a club's forgiveness. Small heads, on the other hand, allow players to manipulate the ball flight more easily. For more consistent ball striking select a larger head. For more control over the flight of your ball select a smaller head.

Fairway woods come in a variety of sizes and shapes. Remember that it is always important to pick something that inspires confidence.

Jargon buster

'Composite' This refers to the design of fairway woods with a graphite crown at the top of a predominantly titanium head.

Selecting the right irons

When it comes to irons, you face making a tricky decision based on the look of the clubs and your own strengths and weaknesses as a golfer. It is all too easy to be wooed into buying a stunning-looking set, but if the clubs are not made to meet your requirements you will be left to rue an expensive mistake. Making a sensible, well-informed choice is therefore imperative. This is what you can expect from the four major iron alternatives.

Blades

Bladed irons have a traditional look with flat backs and thin top-lines, but it can be unnerving looking down on their wafer-thin top-lines at address. Hitting blades successfully requires absolute confidence in the quality of your ball striking. Indeed, it would be fair to say that the strict demands placed on the precision and consistency of your striking puts many players off. However, the benefits on offer for those who can rely on clean contacts are considerable. The ability to manipulate trajectory and ball flight can help you cope with all types of course and conditions.

Shallow cavities

Shallow cavities differ from blades in that the heads are slightly bigger, which makes them marginally more forgiving to off-centre strikes. They offer players a similar blend of good looks and playability to that which you get with blades but with the significant bonus of extra forgiveness. To a certain extent, musclebacks have replaced blades as the most popular choice for many professionals and low-handicap amateurs, because they often look just as classy as blades.

Deep-cavity irons

Because they have wide soles and large heads with hollowed-out sections at the back, deep-cavity irons have a lower centre of gravity than blades and musclebacks, which makes getting the ball airborne easier. The sweet spot should be slightly larger, offering a more forgiving strike. These design benefits help those who feel a little less confident in the precision of their ball striking.

Undercut-cavity irons

Undercut cavities have hollowed-out bottoms. Such a design allows manufacturers to manipulate more precisely where the majority of the weight sits in the head. High-flying shots should be easy to achieve, and with extra weight added to the periphery of the head these irons maximize forgiveness. Undercut-cavity irons are therefore ideal for higher handicappers looking for greater consistency to improve their scores. Their disadvantage is that they do not provide the same playability as musclebacks and blades. They are the bulkiest of the four iron-club types.

Combination sets

Combination sets are a relatively new addition to the iron market and are well worth considering. The idea behind this is to mix shallow cavities in the short irons with deep cavities in the longer clubs. Such a mixture provides forgiveness when you need it the most from long range and playability when you are attacking the green. Combination sets are seen by many as offering the best of both worlds.

Jargon buster

'Playability' The capacity to manipulate the flight of your ball.

'Top-line' The top of the clubhead.

Custom-fitting

Whenever you buy a new set of golf clubs, you do so in the hope that such an investment will bring with it a higher level of performance. It therefore makes sense to find a set to suit your physique and swing. The majority of top manufacturers offer a custom-fitting service for no extra cost, but what exactly does this service involve and how does it ensure that you get the very best from your clubs?

What is custom-fitting?

The basic process involves taking a combination of static measurements and dynamic swing readings to find the perfect formula for each player. By consulting your static height and wrist-to-floor measurements, the custom-fit technician will know the ideal shaft length to suit a player of your build. You will then be asked to hit some shots with these clubs. By attaching impact tape to the face and sole (this marks where the ball hits the face and where the sole of the club hits the ground), the technician can then tweak how the club sits at address. You should then receive clubs that fit perfectly, allowing you to strike the ball from the centre of the blade more often.

What are the benefits?

Golf clubs bought straight off the rack are designed to benefit players of a standard height and build. If you do not fit into these fairly narrow perimeters, the performance characteristics of the clubs will be altered drastically, preventing you from hitting the ball as well as possible. It is in the interests of each manufacturer to sell you a set that performs to its optimum level, and custom-fitting allows them to construct clubs that fit a player's own physique, helping him or her to strike the ball from the middle of the blade more consistently. The recent introduction of launch monitors can help further by customizing your ball flight to maximize distance and accuracy.

Launch monitors

Launch monitors add an extra, hi-tech dimension to custom-fitting and further refines the process. The technician gives you various different clubs to try, and high-speed cameras capture images of the ball and clubface at impact. A computer programme then distils the data generated and provides a list of figures including clubhead speed, launch angle and the rates of backspin and sidespin. The technician will continue to give you different clubs until you start recording an ideal set of readings.

One of the benefits of this process is that you can find a ball flight you feel comfortable with. For instance, if you play the majority of your golf on blustery links courses, you may wish to buy a set that offers a lower, piercing flight to maximize your control.

Selecting your clubs

To record consistently good scores you need a lineup of clubs that helps you make the most of your strengths. But with only 14 clubs allowed in your bag during a game, the decision over exactly what to take on to the course can be tricky. The following advice guides towards building the perfect set for your game, from the numerous helpful technologies on offer.

Woods and irons

When choosing the right combination of woods and irons, there are two important factors to consider.

First, think about the course you are about to play. Is it vast, requiring long approach shots into greens? Or is it tight, placing a premium on accuracy over power off the tee? If the layout is long and open, you will be able to attack the course with a driver and at least two fairway woods. But if the course is lined by trees or thick rough it is important to rely on the clubs that you know will go straight. Replacing a fairway wood or even your driver with an extra-long iron or rescue club should help you avoid trouble.

Second, pick a lineup that will help you play to your strengths. If you find long irons hard to hit, then replace the 3- and 4-irons with easier-to-hit fairway woods or rescue clubs. Alternatively, if you are confident in the quality of your ball striking, long irons are more suitable for shaping the ball through the air to find the fairways.

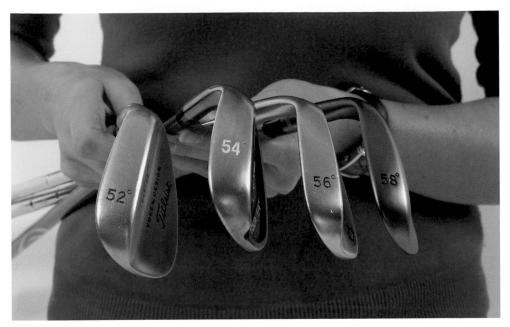

From lob to pitching, choosing the right combination of wedges is crucial.

Wedge game

Many of the professionals on Tour carry four different wedges to help them cope with any situation from around 90 m (100 yards) from the green. You might think this a touch excessive but if you tend to shoot long off the tee a premium will be placed on the quality of your short game, so having a variety of wedge options is crucial. Whether you choose to carry two, three or four wedges will largely depend on the power and accuracy of your long game. Your different wedge options are roughly as follows:

pitching wedge   48-degree loft
gap wedge   52-degree loft
sand wedge   56-degree loft
lob wedge   60-degree loft.

Rescue clubs

Rescue clubs (or hybrids as they are also known) are a relatively recent addition from equipment manufacturers. They combine many of the attributes of irons and fairway woods. With more weight positioned low in the clubhead they are undoubtedly easier to hit than long irons. Their heads are smaller than fairway woods, so they can also be employed in many different situations.

If you find long irons hard to strike well consistently, a rescue club may offer the answer. With many different loft and shaft options available, every golfer should be able to find one that suits his or her game.

THE SET-UP

Most faults in the golf swing can be traced back to problems in the address position. Standing correctly to the ball allows you to swing with poise and power, determining the accuracy and consistency of your ball striking. It is therefore crucial to cement all the key fundamentals before you hit the ball. The following tips help you set up correctly when hitting a driver.

Alignment

It is crucial to ensure that your clubface and body are both aiming in exactly the right direction at address. If your alignment is not perfect it is almost inevitable that your swing will develop serious faults to compensate.

1 Before setting your stance, place your club behind the ball and check to see that the face is pointing directly at your target.

2 Build your stance: your shoulders, hips and feet should all be **parallel** to your ball-to-target line.

Ball position

The position of the ball in relation to your feet can determine both the trajectory and accuracy of the shot, so always pay close attention to this.

When setting up to drive, sit the ball in line with the inside of your left heel. This enables you to sweep the ball away on the upswing for a high trajectory that carries a long way through the air. Modern drivers are designed to offer high ball flights with plenty of carry, so ensure that your ball position allows you to make the most of these important technological benefits.

Weight distribution

In the perfect set-up position, your chin should be slightly behind the ball, and around 70 per cent of your weight should be on your right foot. This encourages an effective weight shift on to your right side as you start the backswing. As long as you drive back towards your left side through impact, a powerful tee shot is guaranteed.

Setting a strong stance

A good athletic stance provides a solid base for a powerful turn. When hitting a driver, position your feet fractionally wider than shoulder width apart and keep your weight on the balls of your feet. This allows you to maintain your balance during the swing. If your weight is in the right position you should be able to lift your heels and then your toes at address without losing your balance.

Jargon buster

'**Alignment**' Refers to where your body and clubface are aiming at address.

'**Carry**' The distance the ball travels through the air before landing.

Iron play at address

Although many of the keys to addressing the ball correctly with your driver remain the same when using irons, there are a few small but crucial differences. By mastering these minor adjustments to your set-up position you will be able to strike the ball cleanly before catching the turf.

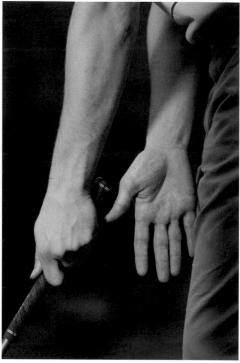

Ball position

The position of the ball in relation to your feet has a huge bearing on the accuracy of the shot as well as the quality of the strike.

When using a mid-iron, move the ball into the middle of your stance. As you drive your arms and body through the downswing, the club will attack the ball from a steeper angle than when using a driver. The arc of your downswing will be more 'v' that 'u' shaped, so your chances of striking the ground before the ball are greatly reduced.

Correct distance from ball

One important consideration about your address position is how far from the ball you should stand. It is important to feel comfortable as you prepare to swing.

To set the perfect position, stand to the ball with a club and let your right hand hang down freely. The butt of the club should be roughly an open hand's width away from your midriff. If you stand too far from the ball you risk striking from the toe, and if you stand too close a shank may result.

Pitching with short irons

When setting up for a short-iron pitch, set a slightly open stance so you have a good view of your target. This helps you deliver an out-to-in swing path to cut across the ball through impact, sending it high into the air.

Jargon buster

'Closed stance' The alignment of your feet and body to the right of the target (for right-handers).

'Open stance' The alignment of your feet and body to the left of the target (for right-handers).

'Pitch' A short shot to the green, usually from inside 90 m (100 yards), which requires the use of a wedge.

Weight distribution

When using a driver, place your weight slightly behind the ball at address and through impact to ensure that you find the optimum launch angle.

When using an iron, there is more loft to play with, so split your weight more evenly and position your hands directly over the ball at address. As you drive the club towards impact, your weight should move on to your left side (see above). This will help you strike the ball before the ground .

Posture

The one thing that every top golfer – regardless of his physical make-up – has in common is a good posture. Standing to the ball with a straight back allows you to swing the club along the right path and consistently strike the ball powerfully from the middle of the clubface. Here is a simple step-by-step guide to building the perfect posture.

Setting the perfect spine angle

1 To establish a good posture, stand upright with your back perfectly straight without flexing your knees. Stand as tall as possible and hold the club out in front of you, as shown.

2 Keeping your knees straight, bend from your hips until your upper body is over the ball, as shown. In this position do not let your shoulders hunch over – keep your back perfectly straight.

3 Relieve the tension in your legs by flexing your knees. Now you are in the correct position. Run through this routine before hitting every shot during a practice session, so you feel comfortable with the correct posture.

The aim of a good posture

Setting a good posture at address allows you to make a powerful upper body turn while keeping the clubhead moving along the right line. If your shoulders are hunched over or you are standing too tall at address, it becomes harder to move your weight effectively through the swing and you risk taking the club back on the wrong line. A good posture is one of the key fundamentals that makes a technically sound swing possible.

Your head should be at the same height immediately after impact as at address – only lift your head after you have allowed the clubhead to release.

Keeping your height

Having set a good posture at address it is crucial to maintain this through impact. If your head dips or rises during the back- or downswing, you will find consistently clean contacts hard to achieve.

Concentrate on keeping your head at the same height until after you have struck the ball. By avoiding unnecessary movements in the swing, the quality of your ball striking is guaranteed to improve.

Jargon buster

'Spine angle' The angle at which your upper body is set in comparison to your lower body, through the swing.

Finishing the swing

After you have struck the ball allow your head to rise as you turn your upper body towards the target. This ensures that your weight moves on to your left side after impact, and the power that is generated during the backswing is carried through impact. Standing tall in the finish position is a good sign of a committed swing.

grip

A reliable grip enables your hands to combine effectively through the swing, returning the clubface square to the target through impact. Quite simply, your hold of the golf club determines how accurate you are so it is a key fundamental that every player should monitor regularly. This step-by-step guide will help you construct an orthodox Vardon grip.

Vardon grip

1 Place your left hand on the club, ensuring that your thumb points down the middle (or fractionally to the right) of the shaft. The top of the club should run from the fleshy part at the bottom of your hand diagonally to the base of your forefinger.

2 Move your right hand into position. Either interlock or overlap the forefinger of your left hand with the little finger of your right. Now wrap your right hand over the club, ensuring that the 'v' shape between your thumb and forefinger points towards your right shoulder. If you are not familiar with this grip it will almost certainly feel uncomfortable at first but after spending time hitting balls on the practice range, cementing the right hold, you will become accustomed to the feeling.

Weak and strong grips

If your grip is weak the 'v' between the thumb and forefinger of your right hand will point towards your chin or even your left shoulder. This simple error opens the clubface as you hit the ball, causing a slice.

If your grip is strong your right hand will be wrapped too far underneath the club, causing the face to close through impact and so fire the ball to the left.

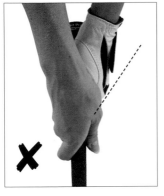

Weak grip.

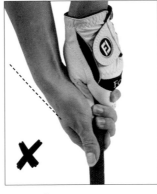

Strong grip.

Interlock or overlap grip

To ensure that your hands combine effectively and keep the clubhead on line through impact, players have two options: an interlocking grip or an overlap one. Neither option is better or worse than the other, so simply choose whichever feels most comfortable for you.

An interlocking grip places the little finger of your right hand between the index and forefinger of your left hand. An overlapping grip places the little finger of your right hand over the index finger of your left hand.

Grip pressure

The simple rule about grip pressure is that you need to hold the club firmly enough for the shaft not to slip or twist in your hands as you strike the ball yet softly enough for your forearms to remain relaxed through the swing. Many amateurs fall easily into the trap of gripping the club too tightly in their endeavour to increase control of the clubhead, but this has a detrimental effect, destroying rhythm and restricting the fluidity of the swing.

Interlocking grip.

Overlapping grip.

Grip checks

Every player should monitor his or her grip regularly to ensure that this is not the cause of destructively wayward shots. To test whether your hands are in the correct place, follow these simple techniques.

Left-hand check

To check the position of your left hand, remove your right hand from the grip and hold the club out directly in front of you. Now remove all of your fingers from the grip apart from your forefinger. If your left hand is in the correct position the clubhead will not fall to the ground. The end of the club will be wedged between the fleshy pad at the bottom of your hand and your forefinger. If the clubhead drops to the ground, you have a poor left-hand grip, which will adversely effect your accuracy.

Initial check

To assess your grip, cock your wrists to lift the club vertically, as you would during the backswing. If this movement is awkward and restricted you need to run through the following checks. A good grip allows your wrists to hinge effectively at the right moments in the swing. If your hold is weak or strong, the amount that your wrists will hinge will be restricted.

Right-hand check

It is crucial that your right hand is in the correct position as this determines exactly when the club releases the ball through impact. To test this, place a tee peg in the 'v' between the thumb and forefinger of your right hand. In the correct position the tee should point towards your right shoulder. If the bottom of the peg aims towards your chin your grip is weak and sliced shots are probable. Alternatively, if the tee points wide of your right shoulder, the grip is strong and you are likely to hit the ball to the left.

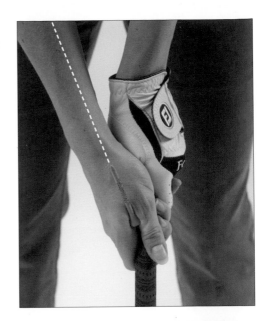

Checking both hands

There are various areas on both hands that you should be able to see clearly before hitting the ball, and you can use these reference points (shown here) while on the course. With your hands in the correct position, you should be able to spot the top two knuckles on your left hand as well as one knuckle on your right. Mark up a glove with the left-knuckle reference point, to provide a guide as you hit balls on the range.

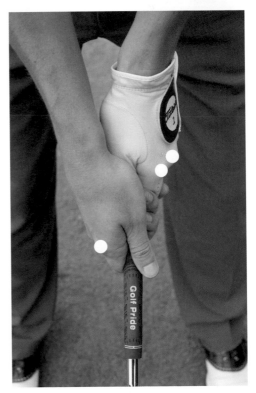

Pressure gauge

It it is easy to hold the club too tightly when you feel stressed. This, however, will only restrict your swing. To check your grip pressure, remove your glove and look at your knuckles as you hold the club. If your grip is too tight, your knuckles will turn white. In this situation, loosen your hold and your knuckles will return to their normal colour.

Building the perfect stance

If you have ever been to a professional Tour event you will doubtless have noticed just how careful the players are when addressing the ball. This highlights how important this part of the game is. The following simple routines are used regularly by some of the best players in the world to check the key fundamentals of ball position and alignment. They can also help you to improve your accuracy on the practice range and the course.

On the practice range

To check that your alignment and ball position are correct, you will need two shafts. Place the first shaft on the ground so it is parallel to your ball-to-target line. This provides a helpful visual reference to ensure that your feet, hips and shoulders are all perfectly square to the target. Now lay the second shaft on the ground at right angles to the first. This marks your ball position. With a driver or fairway wood in hand, the shaft should sit just inside your left heel. When playing with an iron (see left), the shaft (and ball) should lie in the middle of your stance.

Ball-to-target line

If you are unsure whether you are aiming at the target, go over this routine at the practice range. Place your club on the ground with the shaft resting against the toes of both feet. Now walk away and check where the shaft is aiming. Your feet should be parallel to your ball-to-target line and so the shaft should be pointing fractionally left of the target.

Jargon buster

'Ball-to-target' A dead-straight line between your ball and the target.

On the course

It is important to check that these fundamentals are in place before hitting any shot while on the course.

1 To build a good stance, stand to the ball with your feet together (the inside edges of your feet should aim directly at the middle of the ball) and carefully check that the club is pointing directly at your target. A couple of quick glances between these two points will help you aim the face correctly. Now that the clubface is in the right position, focus on your feet.

2 If you are using a driver, simply move your right foot away from your left until your stance is wide enough to provide a solid base for the swing. This ensures that the ball is in the middle of your stance.

3 Now take one last look at the target before pulling the trigger.

SWING PATH

Now that you have set a technically sound address position it is time to focus on the path of your swing. The good news is that your hard work on the set-up should make it easier to hone a good swing movement. This chapter explains how the club should travel through the swing to return the face square to the target through impact and then reveals how to master the perfect swing path.

The right move

A good golf swing requires your arms to move freely, around your body. The clubhead travels up and down along an arc; it does not move in a straight line.

Shape of your shot

There are no real hard-and-fast rules regarding the swing path. Many players have a 'shape' of shot to rely on that comes from a variation on the classic in-to-out plane. Colin Montgomerie, for example, is famed for the gentle fade that has helped him find fairways and greens throughout his career. Padraig Harrington, however, prefers to rely on a right-to-left, drawing ball flight. If you can find a shape that you can trust – especially when the pressure is on – it is not worth changing your swing path in search of a straighter ball flight.

To deliver the face square through impact and hit the ball without sidespin you need to attack the ball from fractionally inside the ball-to-target line. Successfully adopting this movement to your muscle memory is the key to accuracy with your driver, fairway woods and irons.

Picking the right path

The ideal position of the club halfway through the downswing should be as shown here (below left). From such a line you can complete your upper body turn and return the clubface square to the target through impact. If the clubhead is outside the ball-to-target line when halfway through the downswing, you will play a slice (below centre). To make a good strike from such a position you are forced to cut across the ball, creating left-to-right spin at impact. If the clubhead becomes trapped behind your body halfway through the downswing, you will be forced to release your hands early to avoid blocking the ball out a long way to the right (below right). A hook will be the most likely outcome.

Ideal position through downswing.

Clubhead outside ball-to-target line.

Clubhead trapped behind body.

Tape your swing

Checking the path of your swing is virtually impossible without the help of a video recorder. Set the machine up behind you, so that it points directly at your target. Now hit a series of practice shots. Play the tape back and you should see the line on which your club attacks the ball through the downswing. This should help you find the cause of persistently wayward shots.

Jargon buster

'Slice' A common faulty shot that sends the ball spinning off high and to the right.

'Swing path' The route of the clubhead as it travels around the player's body.

'Hook' A destructive shot that sends the ball flying low to the left with right-to-left spin.

'Release' The moment in the swing just after impact when your wrists hinge and elbows extend, enabling you to drive through to the finish position.

The takeaway

If you can set the clubhead moving along the correct path during the first phase of the swing, an accurate shot becomes all the more likely. The speed of your takeaway also has a huge bearing on the rhythm of your swing as a whole. This is the time that it takes from the start to the finish of your swing and it should not differ drastically between woods and irons. Honing a smooth, technically sound first movement is crucial to good play.

Wrist hinge

Your wrists act as levers during the swing, adding to your clubhead speed. They should ideally start to hinge as the club reaches about knee-height on the backswing and then hinge again through impact as you release the clubhead towards the target. Always ensure that you do not hinge your wrists too soon, as shown here (left) during the backswing.

If you snatch the club away by cocking your wrists you risk throwing the clubhead off line; you will also find it hard to move your weight smoothly on to your right side during the backswing.

Power source

At the start of the swing you need to take the club back as far away from the ball as possible in a one-piece takeaway, before you allow your wrists to hinge. Think of this as a sweeping motion and the result will be a wide arc. If the arc of your swing is wide, the clubhead will travel farther, building momentum as it goes. Also as your hands take the club away from the ball you should start to feel that your weight is moving on to your right side. The advantages of a long, wide takeaway will help you hit the ball both straighter and farther.

Straight backward swing

So often the success of your swing will be determined by its first movement. The takeaway is a simple motion and it is important that you do not add any unwanted and unnecessary movements. Concentrate on taking the club back on a natural path. If you start the club moving drastically outside or inside the ball-to-target line, you will be forced to compensate later in the swing, making wayward shots more likely.

Two-ball drill

To groove a smooth, wide takeaway place an extra ball behind your clubhead at address. Practise sweeping this ball away smoothly on a straight line away from the target. This drill is designed to groove a technically sound takeaway that sets a good tempo and an effective swing path.

Jargon buster

'One-piece takeaway' The movement of your hands (without breaking your wrists) away from the ball at the start of the swing.

The transition from the top of your backswing to the start of your downswing needs to be as smooth as possible to maintain the synchronization of your arms and body. It also has to be powerful as it triggers the build-up of clubhead speed towards the critical moment of contact. The following advice will help you master such a transition.

Casting

Casting is a destructive movement caused by throwing your arms away from your body at the start of the downswing. It is a very common fault among amateurs, and it destroys the power created by a good, upper-body turn during the backswing. By flicking your wrists to send the clubhead away from your body at the start of the downswing (above), your arms and body will stop working together effectively. Loss of power and accuracy is the inevitable result.

Your hands should instead drop straight down as you move your hips towards the target. This movement creates lag in the shaft, which is a sign of a genuinely powerful start to the downswing.

'Bumping' your hips

An effective swing thought that will help you trigger a technically sound start to the downswing is to 'bump' your hips towards the target. This entails pushing your hips to the left to trigger the second rotation of your body. This simple but powerful movement creates room to drop your hands so that your arms and body can rotate effectively together through the downswing. Practise swinging back and then 'bumping' your hips towards the target without going any further through the swing. This drill familiarizes you with the correct movement.

Over-swinging

If the club travels as far as parallel to the ground at the top of your backswing, you will be well set, ready for a strong drive through the downswing. Many great players, however, over-swing. John Daly, Phil Mickelson and Colin Montgomerie all send the clubhead way past parallel at the top of the backswing (see right), but they have all developed a swing that they can control as well as maintain their balance for consistently clean strikes. A long backswing is not necessary for a powerful strike and can often be responsible for destroying the synchronization of your arms and body.

Under pressure

When you are under pressure, adrenaline and nerves can provoke you into starting the downswing too soon. This is a common mistake that destroys your rhythm and prevents your arms and body from working in harmony. In this situation, concentrate on completing your backswing by making a full upper-body turn.

Jargon buster

'**Lag**' The bending of the shaft as your hands drive quickly through the downswing.

Angle of attack

The angle at which your clubhead attacks the ball during the downswing determines the quality of the strike as well as the trajectory of the shot. There is a small difference between this ideal angle when using a driver and when you are hitting an iron. Once you have mastered these subtle variations you will become a more complete player, able to get the most from every club in the bag.

Sweeping strike

When using a driver or fairway wood, the ideal angle of attack is shallow. This enables you to sweep the ball off the tee or off the top of the deck to achieve the optimum launch angle and so maximize the distance the ball carries through the air. When hitting woods, try to clip the ball cleanly away without taking a divot.

As well as positioning the ball forward in your stance (see pages 26–27), it is also important to ensure that your weight remains slightly behind the ball through impact. With your head also behind the ball, the club will approach the ball on a shallow arc.

(above right) A shallow 'U-shaped' swing arc allows you to hit the ball powerfully on the up.

(right) To help achieve a shallow swing arc, keep some weight behind the ball through impact.

Downward hit

When playing with an iron, you need a steeper angle of attack to ensure that you make contact with the ball before the turf. Through impact your weight should move over the ball as your body turns back towards the target. However, it is important here to make sure that your weight does not move too quickly on to your left side. If your body is ahead of the ball, your angle of attack will be too steep and a thin contact will produce a low shot, which is impossible to control.

A note of caution

Although when using woods your weight needs to be slightly behind the ball through impact, it must still transfer towards your left side. If your weight gets stuck on your back foot, you risk hitting the ground before the ball.

Jargon buster

'Trajectory' The angle at which the ball leaves the clubface at impact.

Short irons

Many players prefer to move the ball towards the back of their stance when hitting with short irons. A slightly steeper angle of attack ensures that your hands are ahead of the ball through impact. As well as guaranteeing that you strike the ball before the turf, such a position allows you to control the trajectory and prevents the extra loft from making the ball fly too high into the air. In blustery conditions use your wedges, for a lower ball flight.

Drills for a good swing path

Swinging consistently along a technically sound path will improve your accuracy as you find a straighter ball flight. Here are three tips each designed to groove an effective swing plane and improve your radar.

Swinging around your body

Always swing the club around your body on an arc (see pages 28-29). To encourage the ideal movement, imagine that you are hitting a ball off a 3ft (1m) high tee peg. This forces you to make a full upper-body turn, swinging the club around your body on a flatter arc. By far the most common fault relating to the swing path is to attack the ball from too steep an angle – this usually leads to a slice.

Stick with the change

If you are altering the path of your swing, it will feel totally alien at first. Poor shots are inevitable and can make you feel that your game is in a desperate state. But if you have made a decision to change your swing you should persevere; do not let wayward shots demoralize you. Once you become accustomed to the new movement, you will reap the benefits of this hard work and you will become a far better player in the long run.

Through the gate drill

Place two soft objects diagonally either side of the ball, as shown here. This marks the ideal gateway through which the clubhead should move on the perfect, in-to-out swing path. Hit some practice shots swinging the club between these objects. The aim here is to hit 20 balls without touching either gatepost. If the club disturbs either gatepost, you should go back to the start of the routine. Once you have hit 20 consecutive clean shots you can be confident that you have cemented a technically sound, in-to-out path.

A note of caution

Changing your swing path can be difficult and it requires some serious practice. If you have a reliable shape of shot that stems from an alternative to the classic in-to-out path, it might be worth sticking with it and not upsetting your game in search of perfection.

Post drill

This drill is designed to help you set the club moving along the right path through two important phases of the swing. Place a 3ft (1m) tall post vertically in the ground about 3ft (1m) behind the clubhead in line with the target at address. Swing slowly, without hitting a ball, aiming to miss the outside of the post on the backswing and the inside of the post as you return to the impact area. This will clearly illustrate how the club needs to move through the swing to deliver the face square to the target, without creating sidespin through impact. Once you feel comfortable with this movement, remove the post and hit some balls for real to see the effect of this work on your ball flight.

RHYTHM AND TIMING

Why is it that some players make the notoriously taxing game of golf look so easy? Ernie Els, for example, is renowned for having an effortless swing that still produces arrow-straight, booming 275-metre (300-yard) drives. His success is largely built on a sublime rhythm that allows his arms to combine effectively with the rotation of his body. The result is consistently accurate, well-timed shots. This chapter reveals the keys to setting a smooth tempo, and they are guaranteed to raise your performance level.

At impact your arms and body should be turning towards the target together.

Why is rhythm so important?

A good swing tempo is essential for several reasons. First, your rhythm largely determines how accurate your shots are. If the pace of your swing remains under control, your arms and body are more likely to work effectively together to return the clubface square through impact.

Second, a good tempo ensures that the clubhead is moving at its fastest through impact. An efficient build-up of energy during the swing helps maximize the distance you hit with each club in the bag.

Finally, a smooth rhythm helps you remain balanced throughout the swing and improves the quality of your ball striking.

Pace maker

If you are struggling for timing or accuracy on the course, it is always worth checking the speed of your swing. A fast, uncontrolled movement is a major reason behind poor ball striking. However, you should be careful not to reduce the pace too much. If you swing too slowly, you risk destroying the synchronization between your arms and body. The result will be weak, wayward shots that end up doing even more damage to your score.

Timing drill

If you feel your swing speeding up on the course and your technique becoming slightly ragged, this drill will bring it back under control.

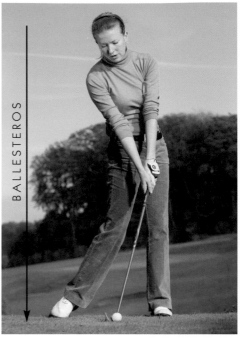

1 As you start your takeaway say the words 'Severiano'. By the time you have said these words you should have reached the top of your backswing.

2 As you begin your downswing say 'Ballesteros'. If you utter the 's' of 'Ballesteros' just as you make contact with the ball you will have swung with an ideal, steady build-up of pace.

Eyes shut drill

It is often said that, if one of your senses is removed, the others become more sensitive. You can apply this theory to your golf swing to check your rhythm. Close your eyes and make a normal swing, as if hitting a shot for real. You should feel completely in control throughout. If you detect that the pace of your swing is causing your weight to move around uncontrollably or you have to take a step to steady yourself at the end, it is a good sign that you need to slow down.

Balance

Because it lies at the heart of clean, powerful ball striking, balance is a critical aspect of a successful swing. Developing a feel for how fast you can swing without losing control will make you a far more potent competitor. The following drills and tips are designed to improve your poise throughout the swing.

A smooth swing should result in a balanced finish position, from which you can watch the ball land.

If you need to take a step to steady yourself, you need to slow the pace of your swing.

Watch it fly

If you have made a smooth swing you should be able to hold your finish position until the ball lands.

However, if you are unable to retain this stance for more than a couple of seconds, your unbalanced movement means that a clean strike is purely a matter of chance. Holding your finish position is an effective swing thought that should trigger a perfectly controlled movement when you are on the course. If you find this impossible to do, make a series of practice swings, gradually reducing the pace of your swing until you can hold your finish position for around ten seconds.

Bare feet drill

An excellent drill popularized by the great American Sam Snead is to hit practice shots without wearing any shoes or socks. As the soles of your feet are in direct contact with the grass, you get a far better feel for how your weight moves during the swing.

At address, place your weight on the balls of your feet, then as you take the club back move it on to your right foot. Through the downswing, drive your weight on to your left side. This drill exposes these weight shifts and will highlight your own sense of balance.

Feet together drill

A classic drill that highlights just how balanced you are is to hit some shots with your feet together. Having a narrow stance destabilizes you, and if you are at all unbalanced at any stage during the swing you will be forced to take a step to steady yourself. If this is the case, simply slow the pace of the swing until you feel confident that you are in control.

Jargon buster

'Finish position' The point at which your body stops rotating and your arms cease moving, after you have hit the ball.

'Flat-footed' You will be said to be flat-footed if you fail to transfer your weight during the swing.

Athletic swing

Maintaining your balance is crucial but you still need to turn your body and shift your weight athletically during the swing. If you are wanting to improve your poise make sure that it does not come at the cost of your athleticism. If you suddenly become flat-footed, you may end up doing more harm than good to your technique.

Swinging in harmony

Every golfer knows just how fragile their form on the course can be. Without feeling that your swing has changed, the difference between one day and the next can easily be ten shots. This is both the appeal and frustration of the game. But there are ways to improve your consistency. By honing a repeatable swing that maintains the synchronization between your arms and body, you will become a more reliable competitor.

The synchronized swing

1 A good swing is a fusion of energy created by your arms and your body. If the two combine effectively, it is a recipe for accuracy, power and clean ball striking. During the ideal movement, your hands and midriff should point in the same direction through the impact area.

2 After impact your hands and midriff should both point towards the target, as shown above.

Jargon buster

'Turn over' To rotate your wrists through impact, causing the clubface to close and the ball to fly to the left.

Movement problems

If you try to hit the ball too hard in search of extra distance it is always likely that your body will rotate too quickly, leaving your arms behind and causing you to leave the clubface open (top). In this situation, preventing the ball from flying way to the right is almost impossible.

Alternatively, if you are lazy about the rotation of your body, a hook is the most likely result (above). Your wrists will turn over too early, causing the clubface to close and creating dangerous left-to-right spin at impact.

Half-shot drill

It is always worth checking the synchronization of your hands and body whenever you get the chance to practise. A good drill to promote correct movement is to hit a series of half shots with a 9-iron. A shorter swing will help you monitor your synchronization. When you feel that your arms and body are combining effectively, gradually lengthen your swing for each ball you hit. By the time you reach your normal full swing, your arms and body should be moving in perfect harmony.

On-course fix

If wayward shots are ruining your round, try this drill on the course without hitting a ball. As you prepare to play, make a series of half swings, ensuring that your hands and body are working together through impact.

Drills for better ball striking

When plotting your strategy for any particular course, you do so in the expectation that your ball striking will be clean. However, occasionally, hitting the ball from the middle of the blade can feel like finding a needle in a haystack. Here are three drills guaranteed to help you find the centre once more.

Jargon buster

'Fat shot' A weak shot that comes up woefully short of its target because the clubface has struck the ground before the ball.

'Heel' The end of the clubface nearest to the shaft.

'Thin shot' A destructive, low-flying shot that occurs when you strike the equator of the ball with the leading edge of the clubface.

'Toe' The end of the clubface farthest from the shaft.

Tee drill

Perhaps the most common reason behind poor striking is altering your spine angle through the swing. A good posture set at address needs to be maintained until after you have struck the ball (see pages 18–21). If you have been suffering with thin or fat strikes in particular, it is worth working on your posture through the swing.

To do this, tee a ball up a couple of inches and hit a series of smooth practice shots with a 9-iron. The only way to clip the ball cleanly off the top is to maintain your spine angle.

Wet sand drill

Seve Ballesteros was famed for his imaginative and instinctive game, which yielded two Masters and three Open victories. As a boy, growing up in Santander, Seve would practise hitting shots on the beach with a 3-iron. This inadvertently honed precise, reliable ball striking.

If your timing is letting you down, find a practice bunker, pour a bottle of water on to the sand and hit some mid- or long-iron shots. If the club catches the sand fractionally too early it will lose all speed and the ball will come up woefully short of its target. A crisp contact is harder to achieve when playing from wet sand, and once you have mastered it you will reap the rewards when you get to the course.

Through the corridor drill

If you have been striking the ball from either the heel or the toe of the club, this drill helps you solve the problem.

Place two soft objects either side of your ball, fractionally wider than a club width's apart – we have used headcovers. Hit a series of practice shots without touching either of these objects. At first you might find this hard to do, but you should soon develop a feel for how to alter your swing to make a clean contact. Hit as many practice shots as it takes to hone consistently precise contacts from the middle of the clubface.

Preparing your swing

Making a smooth swing on the range while the pressure is off is one thing but maintaining this rhythm when a good score rests in the balance on the course is quite another matter. As your heart rate rises and adrenaline flows through your veins, the natural reaction is to swing faster and harder. But this will lose you control. Here are five tips to use just as the pressure mounts. They are guaranteed to help you keep your tempo and deliver a clean strike.

Copy the best

Ernie Els is famed for having a smooth, easy rhythm, so why not copy his style if you are feeling under pressure?

Stand behind your ball and visualize Els' easy-going movement. Now make a practice swing replicating his tempo. This simple tip will relax your muscles and prevent any jerky, unnatural movements from hampering the quality or accuracy of your ball striking.

Controlled breathing

If you can control your breathing, you can prevent the build-up of nervous tension and adrenaline from causing a ragged swing.

Just before you address the ball, stand back and take three deep breaths, exhaling as slowly and for as long as possible. You will start feeling the tension in your body fade away as you begin to relax. Add this process to your pre-shot routine and you will be able to deliver a free-flowing swing even when a good score lies in the balance.

Grip pressure

If your forearms are tense as you prepare to take the club back, a jerky swing becomes the most likely outcome. But you can prevent this destructive build-up of tension by loosening your hold of the club. Monitor the pressure of your grip by using the following scale.

If ten is the tightest that you can possibly hold the club and one is barely strong enough to lift it upright, your ideal grip pressure should be about four on the scale. This allows you to remain in control of the clubhead while making a rhythmical swing.

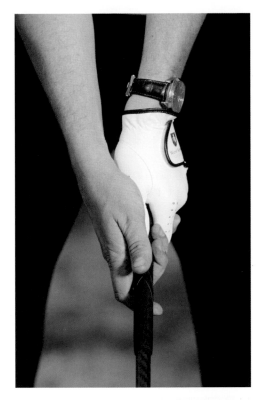

Tip from the Tour

Another simple tip that helps to relieve tension in your forearms is to hover the clubhead just above the ground at address. This is a technique used by some of the best players in the world to relax their forearm muscles in a bid to trigger a smooth swing.

Ready to fire

Once you have addressed the ball and taken a final glance at your target, do not hesitate before taking the club back. The longer you wait here, the more tension starts to build up and the more likely you are to make an unnatural movement.

TURNING YOUR BODY

The golf swing is a dynamic movement that requires a full upper-body turn and an effective weight shift. Think of these movements as the engine room of your swing; they are responsible for much of the clubhead speed that you deliver through impact. Mastering these techniques is vital to the success of your long game. This chapter reveals how to use your body to advantage, and it highlights the most common mistakes and their cures.

Shifting your weight

Your body weight can be a powerful tool, adding power to your golf swing but only if used correctly. As you take the club away at the start of the backswing, gradually move the majority of your weight on to your right side. At the top of the backswing, your chin should be directly over your right foot. Do not be afraid to allow your head to move laterally during the swing, to trigger an effective weight shift.

The coil

Generating enough clubhead speed to deliver a strong ball flight depends on how well you employ your core muscles during the swing. The resistance between your upper and lower body at the top of your backswing adds force to your downswing.

In the ideal position, your back should point directly at the target. As your hips are unable to turn quite so far, you will generate resistance between your upper and lower body. To promote a powerful turn, concentrate on rotating your upper body until your back faces the target.

Driving through

Having set your weight on to your right side at the top of the backswing, it is time to drive powerfully towards your left through impact. In the finish position, your chin should be over your left foot. This is evidence of an effective weight shift on to your left side and a committed swing.

Jargon buster

'Coil' The rotation of your body during the backswing, which creates torque between your upper and lower body.

Stepping drill

Driving your weight towards the target as you hit the ball is a crucial movement that many players struggle to master, because it requires an unwavering trust in the loft of the club to get the ball airborne. The following drill will help you commit this movement to memory.

Place your feet together and make a soft, three-quarter swing. As you drive through the downswing allow your left foot to step towards the target. This also forces you to move your weight towards the target, into the shot. When you see just how the loft of the club works to get the ball airborne, you should be convinced that you do not need to use your body to help.

Leg action

A solid leg action is important to maintain your poise through an athletic swing. This is an area that requires careful consideration and commitment to master, and the following pages demonstrate how to use your legs effectively in different situations during the swing.

At address

Good balance is crucial to the quality of your ball striking (see pages 40–41), and a strong stance provides a stable base for a dynamic swing. At address make sure that there is some 'give' in your knees. This will allow you to transfer your weight and rotate your body without losing control. The stability of your swing depends on the strength of your stance so make sure that you feel comfortable and that there is a reasonable amount of flex in your knees.

Which cleats?

The spikes on the soles of your golf shoes are there to aid your stability and balance through the swing. You can choose between metal spikes and 'soft' plastic ones that were designed to cause less damage to the course, in particular the greens. Most players find that soft spikes provide them with sufficient stability but if during the winter the conditions are particularly soggy it might be worth switching to metal spikes to provide you with a slightly firmer footing.

At impact

Through impact your body should turn towards the target as your arms drive through the downswing. It is crucial that your legs provide the resistance against which your body can rotate. In the ideal position your left knee should be straight, allowing your hips and chest to turn towards the target. If your left knee bends and slides, you will lose power in your swing.

At the finish

By the time you have completed your swing you should be able to feel the majority of your weight loaded on to your left side. In the perfect finish position your right knee should point towards the target with your right heel off the ground. Despite only having your right toe resting on the turf, this is still a balanced position, which you should be able to hold until the ball has landed.

Clean cleats

It is important to have clean spikes, as muddy spikes can cause your feet to slip, badly affecting your swing. Spikes should also be changed regularly, as worn spikes cause instability, which can lead to a flat-footed swing.

Committing to the strike

When you are faced with a narrow fairway flanked by trees on either side or a green surrounded by sand and water, it can be hard to make a naturally fluid swing. If you try to steer the ball towards its target, the resulting swing often lacks conviction and you end up prodding your ball towards the exact trouble you were so desperate to avoid. So even when the situation is intimidating the following advice will help you commit to your normal swing.

An attempt to steer the ball towards its target can result in a swing that lacks conviction.

After impact, keep your elbows straight and turn your right hand over your left to ensure a committed swing.

Full extension

One of the most important movements in the golf swing comes after you have hit the ball. This might sound strange, but the extension of your arms determines the angle of the clubface through impact. In the perfect, post-impact position your elbows will be straight and your right hand will have turned over your left. Your right heel should be fractionally off the ground as you drive your weight towards the target.

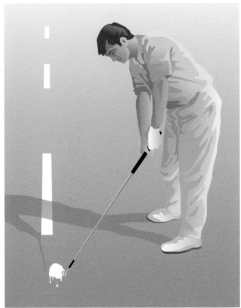

Mopping drill

To perfect the post-impact arm extension, try the following drill.

Take a mop and sweep the floor across your body from right to left. The only way to keep the brushes of the mop on the floor as you move left is to extend your arms as fully as possible (allow your right heel to lift off the ground in this position to aid the extension).

Practise this several times and then copy the movement with a golf club in hand. This drill helps you hone a committed drive of your arms and body through impact.

On-course drill

When you are faced with an intimidating shot that requires a committed movement, make a practice swing imagining that your clubhead is dripping with paint. As you extend your arms away from your body through impact, picture the paint leaving a long, straight line on the ground. Now, as you prepare to hit, concentrate on making a full extension after impact; this should prevent destructive thoughts about the trouble surrounding the fairway from entering your mind and causing a defensive stroke.

Steering the ball

Amateurs are often guilty of trying to steer the ball towards the target when they are desperate for an accurate flight. This is a classic sign of failing to commit to the shot, and the results can be devastating. If you attempt to guide the clubhead through impact you end up pulling your arms into your body and holding the face fractionally open. Without turning your wrists over you are likely to miss the fairway to the right.

Common mistakes and cures 1

Every golfer knows just how difficult finding a reliable swing can be, especially when trying to build a score on the course. In a bid to hit the ball straight to the fairway or green, you may often attempt to be too precise. This can result in failing to use your body effectively during the swing.

Using your weight incorrectly

If you have been failing to shift your weight effectively during the swing, this drill will promote the correct movement. Repeat this drill ten times, then hit a ball for real and you are guaranteed to notice how beneficial an effective weight transfer can be.

Cure: step drill

1 Address the ball with a mid-iron, and as you take the club back lift your left foot off the ground. This forces your weight on to your right side.

2 Now as you drive through the downswing put your left foot back down on the ground, lifting your right foot after impact. In the finish position, your weight will be perfectly set on your left side.

Becoming too static

There are many myths relating to the golf swing. Perhaps the most common misunderstanding is that you have to keep your head still. While it is important not to lift or dip your head, there are no rules against lateral movement.

Cure: allow your head to move

If you are concentrating too hard on keeping your head still to see the strike, this may affect the extent to which you use your weight. Your swing will become flat-footed lacking dynamism and power.

Do not be afraid to let your head move fractionally to the right as you take the club back and then to the left as you drive through. This helps you commit to a full upper-body turn and an effective weight shift.

Turn-and-coil problems

This drill is designed to promote a full upper-body turn and at the same time will also help you feel the resistance between your upper and lower body at the top of the backswing.

Cure: resistance drill

Hit some practice balls with a mid-iron but make one crucial alteration to your address position. Move your right foot forward about 25 cm (10 in), as shown. In this position, make sure that your shoulders and clubface are still aiming at the target (it is often a natural reaction for them to point left here). Take the club to the top of the backswing, completing your body rotation so that your back faces the target. If you hold this position, you should feel the strain between your upper and lower body. This is the coil that will add power to your downswing without costing you control.

Common mistakes and cures 2

Perhaps the most common mistake among amateurs is to reverse pivot. This is a destructive mistake relating to the way that you use your weight during the swing, and the effects can be devastating. These pages explain exactly what a reverse pivot is and also show how you can stamp it out of your game.

With you weight on your left side you'll find it hard to make a sweet strike.

Hanging back on your right foot through impact is a recipe for thin or fat strikes.

What is a reverse pivot?

Reverse pivot occurs when a player moves his or her weight in the wrong direction during the swing. If you suffer from this problem you will move towards the target as you take the club back and then on to your right side as you swing the club back towards the ball. Through impact, the majority of your weight will be on your right side, and your head is likely to be behind the ball.

The effect that this movement has on the arc of your swing is where the problem arises. With your weight on your back foot, your downswing is too shallow and the clubhead grounds out too soon. It either strikes the turf before the ball, causing a weak, fat shot, or it strikes the ball on the upswing, creating a thin contact. If this movement has crept into your technique, these drills will help.

Cure: weight distribution drill

To check whether you are using your weight correctly during the swing, take your normal set-up position and place a shaft on the ground square to the target inside your right heel. Now hold another shaft across your shoulders and rotate your body to the top of the backswing. If your weight has moved correctly on to your right side, the two shafts should be perfectly parallel. This forces you to move your weight away from the target during the backswing, because, if you do not, the top shaft will be parallel to the middle of your stance.

Cure: improve drive-through

Having mastered an effective weight shift on to your right side at the top of the backswing it is now time to drive towards the target through impact.

Tee your ball up about 4 cm (1½ in) high and hit some mid-iron shots. Aim simply to break the tee as you hit the ball. The only way to do this is to hit 'down' on the ball, driving your weight on to your left side through impact.

Jargon buster

'Grounding out' The lowest point in the line of your downswing that resembles either a 'u' shape or a 'v' shape depending on where the ball is positioned in relation to your feet.

SHOT SHAPING

Once you feel comfortable with the basic mechanics behind a successful swing, you can experiment with shaping your ball flight. The ability to move the ball sideways through the air makes you a more complete player, able to attack tucked-away pins and find fairways that run at an angle to the tee. This chapter guides you through the key movements required to manipulate your ball flight.

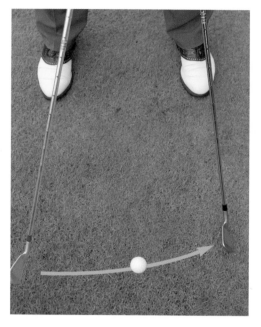

Fade

A fade is a controlled shot that drifts from left to right through the air and has a higher than normal trajectory. This movement is caused by sidespin created at impact. As the clubhead travels along an out-to-in path, cutting across the ball through impact, left-to-right spin moves the ball to the right through the air. The clubface points to the target through impact but the path of the club will cause the ball to start flying left. When hitting a fade expect the trajectory to increase slightly, as the clubface is open (adding loft) in comparison to your body.

Draw

A draw moves the ball in the opposite direction, drifting it from right to left through the air. The club travels on a slightly exaggerated, in-to-out path, and because the face is closed in comparison to the body through impact, right-to-left spin turns the ball to the left. A closed face de-lofts the club, so the ball flies lower and farther than usual.

Setting up for a fade

Hitting a fade or draw might seem complicated but all you need do is make a simple tweak to your address position to alter the path of your swing.

To produce a fade, carefully aim the clubface directly at the target. Now take your stance, ensuring that your feet, hips and shoulders are all pointing to the left of the target. As long as you take the club back along the line of your body, an out-to-in swing path will deliver the desired result.

Setting up for a draw

The opposite rules apply when hitting a draw. Carefully align the face of your club with the target. Now set your stance, ensuring that your feet, hips and shoulders are all aiming to the right of the target. The clubface will be closed in comparison to your body and the resulting, in-to-out swing path creates a draw.

A word of warning

When setting up to hit a fade or draw it is important to grip the club only after you have pointed the face and set your stance. If you grip the club and then open or close the face, you will struggle to square the face through impact and wayward shots are inevitable.

Jargon buster

'Loft' The trajectory of the shot you hit. Different clubs have different loft in order to determine how far the ball travels. The more degrees of loft each club has, the higher the ball will fly and vice versa.

Hitting a fade

A high-flying, soft-landing fade helps you attack pins cut tightly behind water or sand. From the tee a soft cut is handy when you are looking to find a fairway that meanders to the right. And when the wind is blowing from right to left, playing for a fade helps you find a perfectly straight ball flight. To master this shot you need to develop a feel for how the body should move. The following tips should spark an instinctive feel for the shot.

Stance then grip

 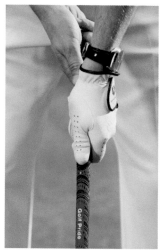 

1 Point the clubface at the target and aim your feet, hips and shoulders left if you want to play a fade (see pages 58–59). After you have taken your stance, take care to ensure that you grip the club properly. Do this by turning the top of the shaft to the right, thereby allowing the clubface to point slightly right.

2 Now take your grip. This might feel strange at first but you will soon start to see how this helps you find the right shot shape. Many players make the mistake of taking their grip and then opening the clubface, but this can lead to a devastating pull.

3 The key to hitting a consistent and controllable fade is to hold the clubface fractionally open through impact. This is the crucial movement that imparts left-to-right spin on the ball. The best way to do this is to hold off your finish by allowing the clubface to keep moving towards the target. Do not let your wrists release as they usually would after impact.

A less technical approach

If the idea of hitting a fade sounds unnecessarily complicated, take five minutes on the range to run through the following pre-shot routine and you should discover how easy the shot is.

Pick a target where you want the ball to finish and aim the clubface directly at it. Now choose another spot about 15 degrees left of it, at which to aim your feet, hips and shoulders. From this alien set-up position, hit a shot. You should have produced a gentle fade.

The idea here is that by aiming your body to the left you can swing the club on the ideal, out-to-in path without thinking about it. The ball will start flying to where your body is aiming and will finish where the clubface is pointing.

Jargon buster

'Cut' The same controlled shot as a fade, where the ball shapes from left to right through the air at a higher than normal trajectory.

'Holding off the finish' When you do not allow your wrists to cock after impact but instead make the club continue moving towards the target. This forces the face to remain slightly open through impact.

Hitting a draw

The ability to hit a draw is a handy weapon that offers the same benefits as a fade (of finding tight pins and awkward fairways) and also the added one of extra distance. The following tips and drills will help you master the perfect movement for a controlled, right-to-left shot. If you devote time to mastering these on the practice range, you will become a more rounded golfer.

Set-up

To address the ball for a draw, point the clubface at your target and now align your feet, hips and shoulders to the right of this mark, as shown. This simple adjustment alters your natural swing path, causing the club to move on a more rounded plane through the downswing. The ball takes off in the direction of where your feet are aiming and finishes on the same line as the clubface. As when you set up for a fade, your body is not supposed to point in exactly the same direction as the clubhead.

Wrist action

The key movement when hitting a draw is to allow your hands to release a fraction earlier than usual. If your wrists start turning as you strike the ball, you impart right-to-left at impact. Spend time practising this movement on the range, because timing it correctly lies at the heart of controlling your draw. If you release your hands too soon a vicious hook is inevitable.

Baseball grip drill

One of the first things you are told when you start playing golf is to ensure that you hold the club correctly. A Vardon grip (see page 22) allows your hands to work together through the swing, improving both your power and accuracy. But when hitting a draw your right hand needs to be in control of the shot, allowing your wrists to break earlier than usual.

To help you understand this movement, try hitting a series of practice shots with a split 'baseball' grip. As your hands are no longer joined together on the club by overlapping fingers, they should start to work independently from each other. This enables your right hand to become more active through the downswing. As your wrists break through impact, the clubface will close slightly delivering a drawing ball flight.

Think 'topspin forehand'

A good analogy that helps illustrate the ideal movement when hitting a draw is to think of a tennis player hitting a topspin forehand. The right hand rotates the racket over the ball, imparting right-to-left spin on the ball. This movement is exactly the same when hitting a draw, so if you need a trigger thought when you are on the course think of a topspin forehand.

Using your honed skills

You can make your time practising on the range enjoyable and worthwhile by experimenting with your ball flight. Hitting a draw or a fade when the pressure is off is the only way to develop the key fundamental movements to manipulate your ball flight. But how do you keep calm when you get to the course and ensure that you deliver the right shot-shape when you need to the most? The following advice is designed to prepare you effectively for the perfect movement.

Visualize the shot

One of the most effective mental devices that helps you deliver just the shot you want is to picture it beforehand. As you prepare to hit a fade or draw, stand behind your ball and visualize the ideal flight. Imagine the ball soaring towards its target and where it would land. This rehearsal establishes a positive mind-set. Because you are totally focused on hitting a good shot, you are no longer worried about trees or bunkers. With the ideal ball flight clear in your mind, your chances of translating this into a good result are vastly improved.

Pre-shot routine

The next time you watch a major golf tournament on television or for real, notice how meticulous the players are over their pre-shot preparations. Each player will have a set routine that helps him or her switch into auto-pilot and forget the pressure of the situation. If you have not already got a pre-shot routine, it is worth using one.

When you are preparing to hit a fade or a draw, the following sequence helps you set a solid address position.

1 Pick two small spots to aim at: one should be where you want the ball to finish – either a specific area on the green or spot on the fairway – and the other should be a mark in the distance on a straight line from where you want the ball to begin its flight. Focus your attention on the branch of a tree or a particular feature on a building in the distance, as this will serve to narrow your aim for greater accuracy.

2 Make your clubface point directly at your target - where you want the ball to finish.

3 Now set your stance, aiming your feet, hips and shoulders where you want the ball to start flying (either to the left or right of your target, depending on whether you are planning to hit a fade or a draw).

TRAJECTORY

Very rarely do you find yourself playing golf in dead calm conditions. Whether you are on a tree-lined inland course or windswept links, there is usually a breeze to contend with, waiting to play havoc with your natural game. This chapter is filled with helpful technical advice designed to give you greater control over the trajectory of the ball. In the wind, these tips will prove invaluable.

Hitting the ball high

When the wind is behind you, or you are planning to attack a pin tightly tucked behind a hazard, you should play a high shot. You can control the trajectory of your shots just by hitting the ball harder or softer. If you hit the ball harder, you create extra backspin at impact, which causes the ball to climb high into the air, but be careful not to unbalance yourself while playing such a shot. All you need do to produce a much higher shot is slightly increase the clubhead speed at impact. A softer swing will reduce backspin for a lower flight.

Hit a fade

A fade will cause the ball to fly higher than usual. If you feel comfortable controlling a fade, then do not complicate matters by doing anything else. Simply set up to the ball with your stance aiming left and the clubface pointing directly at the target (see pages 58–59). This helps you produce a high-flying, soft-landing shot.

If you are looking for a towering ball flight, why not set up to hit a fade?

Jargon buster

'Links' A type of course built on a typically arid stretch of coast. It is so-called because it links the land to the sea.

With your driver

If you feel uncomfortable controlling a fade off the tee, make a slight adjustment to your swing to deliver a higher trajectory. Through impact leave your weight hanging back on your right foot, although the majority of your weight should still be on your left side in the finish position. Your head and hands will be slightly behind the ball, increasing the loft of the clubface. It is important to realize that this is a tricky technical change that requires some careful practice. Only take this shot with you to the course if you have already mastered it on the range.

Tee it high

Tee the ball up slightly higher than usual at address. This encourages you to strike the ball on the upswing for a higher flight. Modern drivers are designed to offer greater carry through the air, so if you increase the trajectory of your drives, longer tee shots become more likely.

Increasing power

The good news for most of us is that you do not need to be a tall body builder to hit a golf ball a long way. Far more important is your technique and flexibility. If the club is moving rapidly through the most important phase of the swing, it inevitably moves the ball an impressive distance away.

Clubhead speed

To increase your power it is essential to swing the club faster. In translating this statement into action many amateurs fall into the trap of increasing the pace of their swing as a whole and so lose control because their arms and body fail to work in harmony.

Downswing

It is only through the impact area that clubhead speed is so crucial. Your hands and arms need to move only a couple of miles per hour faster here to deliver a significant improvement on your overall distance. To generate extra momentum allow your hands to drop at the start of the downswing.

Increasing acceleration

To hone a steady acceleration through the ball, make a series of practice swings with two clubs. The extra weight in the head drives your hands through the downswing, increasing your acceleration. When you hit a ball for real, the club will feel lighter and your hands will move faster as you strike the ball.

Stand firm

Every so often you will be faced with a long, open hole that requires a powerful drive. In this situation you should prepare for a faster swing than usual so your stance should be wider to provide greater stability.

Increase the width of your stance by roughly 30 cm (1 ft) while ensuring that the ball still sits in line with your left heel. Concentrate on completing your backswing before accelerating the club through impact. You should find that crucial extra yards will be achieved without loss of accuracy on the fairway.

Strengthening your core

Professional golfers will often train their core body muscles. A strong back and abdomen will add stability to the swing and strength to your turn, resulting in greater power.

Staying loose

Flexibility as opposed to muscle lies at the heart of powerful ball striking (in fact, people with huge biceps often suffer from a lack of fluidity). Before hitting the ball it is important to relax your forearms so they are ready for a rhythmical movement. If these muscles are tight, the arc of your swing will become restricted and the clubhead will not be moving at its optimum speed through impact.

Prevent your forearms from tensing by waggling the club a couple of times as you stand to the ball at address. Then just before you start the swing, hover the clubhead in the air as shown. These simple pre-shot techniques will help you stay relaxed, preventing the build-up of tension.

Developing the punch

When the fairways are hard and fast or the wind is in your face,
a low-flying punch will optimize the distance and control of
each shot by minimizing backspin and ensuring the ball does
not climb too far into the air. Although mastering this variation
is relatively simple, it does require some careful work on the
practice ground. Here are all the mechanics you need to produce
a successful punch.

Ball position

The position of the ball in relation to your feet at address can
have a huge bearing on the trajectory of the shot (see pages
18–19). If you are planning a lower flight than usual, move the
ball back in your stance a couple of inches and place fractionally
more weight than usual on your left foot. These adjustments
help you find a steeper angle of attack into the ball, de-lofting
the club through impact to deliver a lower, piercing ball flight.

Moving the ball back in your stance will help you
produce a lower ball flight to tackle an oncoming wind.

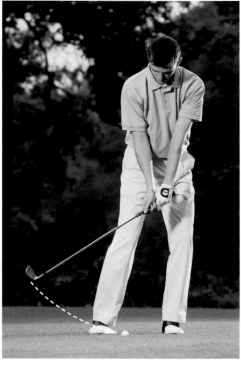

To achieve a steeper angle of attack and minimize loft,
lean your weight slightly onto your left foot at address.

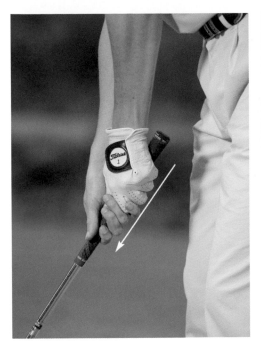

Grip down the shaft

When setting up for a punch, move your hands to the bottom of the grip – almost on the shaft. This not only reduces the length of the club but also restricts the natural fluidity of your swing. In this instance a slightly constrained movement has a positive effect, because it reduces the amount of backspin generated at impact and thus prevents the ball ballooning high into the air.

Follow-through

For any normal shot a full follow-through is evidence of a committed strike, but this can actually work against you when playing a punch. If you are planning a lower flight make sure that your follow-through is shorter than usual. This prevents your hands from releasing too quickly through impact and imparting backspin on the ball.

A note of warning

If you move the ball back in your stance without adjusting your grip, the clubface will naturally sit open. It is crucial therefore that the face is pointing directly at the target before you take your grip and stance. When looking down at address the clubface may feel slightly closed, but this is just an illusion as you are not accustomed to seeing the ball or club so far back in your stance.

Club selection

Because the backspin created at impact has a huge bearing on the trajectory of the shot, it makes sense to swing slightly slower than usual in order to reduce backspin and prevent the ball from climbing too high. When the wind is in your face, take an extra club and swing more softly; what you lose in distance, you gain in control.

Drills for a lower flight

Mastering any variation on your natural ball flight requires careful practice. These drills are designed to make this practice as simple, effective and enjoyable as possible. Without placing too great an emphasis on the specific swing mechanics you should be able to master the punch.

Obstacle drill

Hitting hundreds of punch shots on the practice ground may help you master the technique, but it will not prepare you for the pressure of needing to hit the shot for real. It makes sense therefore to practise hitting balls under an obstacle.

Find a tree with branches that extend about 4 metres (12 ft) off the ground. Place some balls about 9 metres (30 ft) behind the tree and practise firing shots beneath the branches. Start cautiously hitting half-shots to hone the perfect trajectory. Once you feel confident about avoiding the branches, increase the power. By the end, you'll be hitting powerful punches with ease.

Chip-and-run drill

In many ways a punch is an extended version of a chip-and-run shot, so a good way to practise producing a lower flight is to build up towards a full swing from a simple chip.

To play a chip-and-run, move the ball back in your stance and place 70 per cent of your weight on your left foot. Hit 20 balls, allowing your swing to get fractionally longer each time but preventing your wrists from breaking during the swing and adding unnecessary loft to the shot. As you reach a full shot, however, your wrists will need to break during the backswing, but this should not add too much height to the shot.

Jargon buster

'Closed' Refers to the angle of the clubface either at address or through impact when it points to the left, reducing loft either at impact or at address.

'Open' Refers to the angle of the clubface either at address or through impact when it points to the right, thus also adding loft to the face.

'Pre-shot routine' A series of actions that allows you to focus positively on the shot in hand and prepare for a fluid swing.

On-course control

When you are faced with hitting a punch on the course for real, it is important to prevent too many technical thoughts from clouding your mind. Once you have set your address position, squeeze the grip until your knuckles turn white.

Now start your swing as usual without concentrating on any specific mechanics. With a firm grip, your swing will remain compact preventing too much clubhead speed and backspin from being generated at impact.

Shot-shaping and trajectory keys

- To hit a fade, the clubface needs to be open through impact in relation to your body; for a draw it should be closed.

- Take care over your address position, because setting your body to aim in a slightly different direction to the clubface will automatically change your swing path to deliver the desired shape of shot.

- When on the course visualize the ideal ball flight then employ a pre-shot routine for a good result.

- Move the ball forward in your stance for a higher trajectory and take it back for a lower flight.

- Reduce the tension in your forearms at address in order to hit the ball further.

- Make a slightly softer swing to hit the ball lower; swing harder to hit it higher.

- Control the fluidity of your swing (and the backspin generated through impact) through the strength of your grip.

DIFFICULT CONDITIONS

When you compete in strokeplay golf you take on the course far more than your opponent. The challenge that you face is largely dependent on the conditions. On a tough day, the way in which each player copes with the added danger of difficult conditions will determine where they appear on the leaderboard. This chapter guides you towards a more robust swing, which remains under control as the weather deteriorates.

Be prepared

Playing well in poor weather conditions requires careful preparation. Before starting on the course make sure that the spikes on your shoes are clean and not too worn – a firm footing is crucial to maximize your control of the swing. Waterproof clothing, a dry towel, an umbrella and a couple of gloves are also essential.

Playing successfully in the rain requires care to ensure that your hands and grips remain dry. Take shelter under your umbrella and attach your towel to the spokes inside. This is absolutely crucial in helping you dry your grips before each shot. In wet weather, swap gloves every three holes (and remove your glove after each shot, putting it under the umbrella) to ensure that you have a firm hold on the club throughout the round.

Judging the wind

Before you play any shot in windy conditions, it is important to consider the strength and direction of the breeze. Add the following three steps to your pre-shot routine to make sure that there are no surprises in store as you hit the ball towards the target.

1 Grab a handful of grass, throw it into the air and see what effect the wind has. This age-old tactic will prove invaluable in helping you select which club to hit and where to aim.

2 Judging wind speed and direction can be especially difficult when playing a tree-lined course. You can be sure that when the ball reaches the peak of its flight, above the treetops, it will be effected by the wind conditions. So before hitting take a look at the treetops to see which way they are being blown. This will help you decipher the effect of the wind when your ball reaches its highest point.

3 Before hitting an approach shot take a look at the flag to determine the effect of the wind around the green. Regardless of the type of course you are playing – links, heathland or tree-lined inland – you might be hitting from a sheltered area, and such a weather check will stop you being fooled into thinking that there is less wind than there actually is on the green.

Playing in the wet

Few golfers enjoy playing in the rain, but unless there is lightning in the area or the course is waterlogged you will be forced to battle on as usual. Wet weather can play havoc with your balance, badly affecting your swing unless you make a couple of minor adjustments. Here is how to improve your control whenever the ground is wet under foot.

Steep angle of attack

If your ball lies on a wet fairway or in the rough, you need to give it a good strike, which requires a precise contact. So move the ball back in your stance by 5–8 cm (2–3 in). This will help you find a steeper angle of attack than usual, ensuring that you strike the ball first and the turf second. If you catch the turf even just a fraction before the ball, the water in the ground will slow the clubhead, causing a woeful lack of distance.

Changing your grip

Another technique worth employing to raise the bottom of your swing arc, and prevent a heavy contact, is to grip the club tighter and slightly farther down the shaft than usual. These adjustments will restrict your swing to make sure that you nip the ball crisply off the top of the wet turf without taking a divot.

Jargon buster

'Heavy contact' Striking the ground before the ball, thereby reducing clubhead speed through impact and causing the ball to come up short of its target.

'Plug' A ball plugs when it remains in its pitchmark after it lands.

Club selection

Whenever a golf course is wet, the ball will stop quickly or even plug when it lands on the fairway or green. So it is always worth factoring in this lack of roll when selecting which club to hit.

A rescue club will prove an invaluable part of your armoury in wet conditions. Because it features more weight lower in its head, a rescue club is designed to increase your carry through the air while also forgiving off-centre strikes. In contrast, long irons tend to be harder to hit, delivering a lower flight with less carry. If you have not already tried a rescue club, ask your local pro if you can take one out to test on the course. You should immediately see how much easier it is to get the ball away on a good flight than it is using your long irons.

Firm footing

When the ground is wet, it is easy for your feet to slip as you swing, even if you are wearing longer metal spikes, so widen your stance a fraction at address to improve your stability. Rotate your body and employ your weight effectively through a strong leg action to keep your swing as familiar and consistent as usual. It is important here to ensure that setting a firm, wide stance at address does not lead to a flat-footed swing.

Coping with sidehill lies

Golf course architects have always employed changes in elevation
to define and defend their courses. Playing uphill, over a hill or
down towards your target makes judging distances more
problematic. Perhaps the most difficult aspect to an undulating
layout is the prospect of playing from a sidehill lie. To master this
art you need to understand how your lie can affect your strike
and swing path and how to allow for the resulting ball flight.

Ball below feet stance

Make one simple alteration to your
address position. Your posture will
determine the quality of your strike, so,
to ensure that it is a clean one, bend
your upper body over the ball slightly
more than usual. It is important here
that you bend your upper body from the
hips and that your back remains straight
and your knees flexed. At first such a
position may feel alien, but by altering
your posture you can make a normal
swing and expect a sweet strike.

Ball above feet stance

The opposite laws apply when the ball
sits above your feet. Feel as if you are
standing more upright than usual at
address, ensuring that your knees remain
flexed and your back is straight.

In both of these side-slope instances
the posture that you set at address
should not alter before you have struck
the ball, because this will have a
detrimental affect on your swing path
and strike.

Swing paths and ball flights

Whenever you play from a slope your swing path is automatically affected. Because your body is set at a greater angle at address (to maximize your chances of a clean contact), the path of your swing will change, causing the ball to slide sideways through the air. Do not fight this shape but allow for it and you should still be able to hit your target.

Trust the slope

It is important to have absolute confidence that the slope will affect your ball flight. If you fail to align your feet, hips and shoulders at one specific spot (either right or left of your target, depending on the slope) you risk hitting a devastatingly wild shot.

Ball below feet

When the ball is below your feet, your swing will be more upright than usual creating left-to-right spin at impact. It is, therefore, imperative to aim to the left and allow for a gentle fade to bring the ball back to its intended target.

Ball above feet

When the ball is above your feet, your swing will inevitably become flatter, resembling a tennis player's topspin forehand (see page 63). This will cause right-to-left sidespin at impact that moves the ball left through the air. In this situation, aim to the right of your target to compensate for this flight.

Playing from the rough

Whenever you miss the fairway you face an important decision on which club to use to play back from the rough. Do you play aggressively and attack the green as usual, or should you hold back, hitting safely towards the middle of the fairway? Your conclusion will largely be determined by your lie.

From thick rough

When your ball is nestled down at the bottom of some thick rough, your only option is to hack it back on to the fairway. In this situation it is easy to relax at the prospect of a relatively straightforward task. But if your guard slips you'll compound the error by failing to get the ball on to the fairway.

Take a sand wedge and move the ball back in your stance. This will create a steeper angle of attack than usual, which will help you strike the ball before hitting the long grass.

Also, open the clubface fractionally before starting the swing. Long grass can often cling on to the shaft, twisting it to the left through impact. By opening the face at address you prevent the ball from shooting off low and to the left.

Setting the angle

To ensure that the clubhead reaches the ball with enough speed to force it back on to the fairway, you need a steep angle of attack into the ball. Do this by hinging your wrists earlier than usual on the backswing. This movement prevents the club from becoming caught up in the grass before reaching the ball.

Prepare for the strike

You can legitimately test how thick grass affects your swing by making a series of practice swings in similarly dense rough a short distance away from your ball. This helps you gauge just how tough the grass is and how much it will slow the clubhead through impact.

Rules reminder

When your ball is sitting in the rough, you must not bend or press down the grass surrounding it. Some amateurs can occasionally be seen improving their lie by creating a small clearing around the ball but such an action breaks rule 13–2 and will cost you a painful, two-shot penalty.

Club selection

When you are in the rough, your lie is not the only factor that will determine which club you select to play. You also need to consider the dangers that lie ahead on that particular hole. If there is water or sand surrounding the green, choosing a shorter club to lay up is usually the most sensible option.

If the path ahead is relatively clear and your lie is not too bad, a rescue club will help you find the bottom of the ball with enough power for a longer shot.

Coping with crosswinds

There are few more difficult conditions to play in than a brisk crosswind. If the breeze catches your ball, you can only watch helplessly as it veers dangerously away from your intended target towards serious trouble. There are, however, a few tricks that help your ball stay firm in the face of a strong wind.

Left-to-right wind

A left-to-right wind is perhaps the hardest condition to cope with. Such a wind direction can appear to give the right-hand side of the course magnetic properties, and thereby encourages a slice. But in this situation one simple alteration to your address position can help you fight the wind.

Before taking your grip, rotate the shaft to the left. With the face toed-in at address, you generate right-to-left sidespin at impact. This will counteract the effect of the wind, helping you find an arrow-straight ball flight. When employing this technique, aim straight at the target and trust that the change to your grip will deliver the desired result.

Aiming left

If toeing-in the club to hold your ball up in the breeze sounds too complicated, there is a slightly more straightforward alternative technique. Simply aim to the left and let the wind move your ball back towards the target. It is important here to take extra care over your alignment to ensure that you commit to your selected line.

Aim the clubface at one spot to the left of the fairway or green (such as the corner of a bunker). Now take your stance, ensuring that your feet, hips and shoulders are all perfectly square to your new ball-to-target line. Swing with conviction and the wind will bring your ball back towards its target.

Right-to-left wind

Most players prefer a right-to-left wind as such a direction allows you to swing aggressively without fear of carving the ball way to the right. If however, your natural ball flight is a draw, you need to be careful. You can prevent the wind from causing your ball to drift leftwards by delaying the release of the club through impact.

Allow your right hand to turn over your left only after you have struck the ball. Through impact the clubface should remain fractionally open, creating left-to-right spin, which will hold the ball on line in the wind.

Aiming right

If you choose instead to allow the wind to affect the flight of your ball, the same rules apply about aiming right. Pick a spot to the right of your target and build your stance as if you are playing directly towards this point. Swing with conviction, aiming to drive the club to the right of your eventual target.

Jargon buster

'Toed-in' Refers to the position of the clubface at address when the toe is turned slightly to the left. This shuts the clubface, causing the ball to fly slightly to the left of where your body is aiming.

Escaping fairway bunkers

Your heart will inevitably sink as you stand on the tee watching your ball trickle into a fairway bunker. However, if you draw a good lie in a relatively shallow trap, you should still be able to attack the green with confidence. The key to success here lies in the quality of your strike. The following tips help you find the perfect contact so your ball emerges safely and powerfully from sand.

Club selection

The severity of the bunker lip will have a huge bearing on which club you choose to play. Whenever you find sand it is a cardinal sin to leave your ball in it, so getting the ball safely back into play should be your primary concern.

To help you decide which club to play, stand behind your ball and visualize the trajectory that you would expect from each club. Now pick up an iron that you are certain will get you safely over the lip and which will enable you to attack the shot with confidence.

Grip control

By far the most common mistake when playing from a fairway trap is to make a heavy contact, which causes the ball to emerge only a few yards from the bunker. To reduce the risk of hitting the sand before the ball, move your hands down the shaft about 1 in (2.5 cm) more than usual. Also squeeze the grip as hard as you can. Your forearms will tense, reducing the arc of your swing and so helping you clip the ball off the top of the sand without taking an energy-sapping splash.

Firm footing

As you take your stance, shuffle your feet into the sand. This will provide you with a firm footing, ready to make an athletic swing. It will also give you a feel for how soft the sand is. If it is hard under foot, you might be able to get away with taking a small amount of sand through impact. If it feels soft, you need to concentrate even harder on making a crisp contact.

Keeping your height

For a clean strike it is always important to maintain a good posture during your swing (see pages 20–21). However, when playing from sand there is absolutely no margin for error with regards to the strike, so it is worth paying even closer attention to your posture.

1 Make sure that your back is straight at address and that there is a reasonable amount of flex in your knees.

2 Keep your head at exactly the same height through the backswing and down to impact. If you dip it, the club will hit the sand before the ball. Only after you have struck the ball should your head rise as you turn your body towards the target. When attacking the green from a fairway trap have one simple swing thought – keep your height.

Jargon buster

'Lip' The top face of the bunker.

PRE-ROUND PREPARATIONS

Your pre-round preparations should be geared entirely towards ensuring that you are ready to perform to the very best of your ability when you step on to the first tee in competition. If you fail to prepare, it is inevitable that you will end up throwing shots away needlessly. Whether from practice rounds, warm-ups or on the range, this chapter reveals how you can save crucial shots before you even tee off.

Devising a strategy

It is always worth buying a course planner before starting the course, especially if you have never played that particular layout before. Before stepping on to the first tee, take ten minutes to scrutinize the course planner and devise your best route round. Pinpoint where the most dangerous hazards lie and develop a strategy that takes them out of play. Mark on the planner where you want to hit your ball on each hole. This quick and easy exercise helps you devise a positive game plan before your thinking becomes affected by events during the round.

Practice round

If you use practice rounds effectively, you can fine-tune your game ready to take on the course for real. If your ball finds a bad lie on the fairway or around the green, avoid the temptation to reposition it on to a perfect patch of lush grass. By always playing your ball from where it lies you develop your general skills and gain a far better feel for how to cope with certain likely scenarios.

Assessing the damage

After your practice round, move to the range and concentrate on your most persistent faults – whether they are your accuracy from the tee or your ball striking from the fairway. A short period of time devoted to rectifying any problems in your game will pay off when you play the course for real, with a positive mind-set.

Jargon buster

'Course planner' A booklet that you can buy from the pro shop, which features sketches of each hole with distances to the green and significant hazards.

Lay-up area

Part of your preparation for a competitive round should be to determine the best places from which to attack the flag. Whether it is a lay-up area on a par five or long par four, or where you drive to on a short par four, you should hit some practice wedge shots on these holes from a yardage that you feel comfortable with. Find a spot on the fairway from where you can confidently reach the flag – perhaps 55 metres (60 yards) or 110 metres (120 yards) away. Mark this point on your course planner so that when you play that particular hole for real you know where your ideal lay-up area lies.

Warming up

Warming up effectively should be an integral part of every golfer's pre-round preparations. A comprehensive warm-up routine is important for a number of reasons, such as improving your flexibility and strength and ensuring that you remain injury-free. The following stretches loosen up your key muscles so that when you step on to the first tee you are ready to make an athletic swing.

Upper-body stretches
Stretch your upper body comprehensively before playing to ensure that you don't waste a swing.

1 Stand upright with your feet set a shoulder's width apart. Try to link your hands behind your head, as shown. Hold this position, feeling the strain in your arms, for ten seconds. Then shake out your arms and do the same stretch again but swap the position of your arms. This will free up your triceps ready for a rhythmic, fluid swing.

2 Now stretch your upper body by holding your right arm across your body with your left hand, as shown. Feel the strain here for ten seconds. Now do the same with your left arm across your body. Run through this stretch five times to further relieve tension in your arms and back.

Lower-body stretches

Much of the stability and power generated during your swing comes from a strong leg action.

1 To stretch your quadriceps, hold your right foot behind your body, as shown. Remain in this position, feeling the strain in your quads, for ten seconds. Now do the same stretch with your left leg.

2 You can also stretch the back of your legs. Extend your right leg in front of you and, with your heel on the ground, tilt back your foot. Lean gently forward. Hold this position for 10 seconds and feel the strain on your hamstring and calf muscles. Now repeat the stretch with your left leg.

Rotation stretch

When you make a dynamic swing, your core muscles provide stability and power. Before you start on the first tee you must warm up this muscle group rigorously.

Take a club and stand with your feet set a shoulder's width apart. Hold the shaft of the club across the top of your back, as shown. Now mimic your backswing, holding the position at the top for ten seconds. Then rotate your body into the finish position and hold this for a further ten seconds. Run through this sequence five times, so the muscles responsible for a controlled but powerful turn will be ready for action.

Working through the bag

If you get the opportunity to attend a European Tour event, you will notice how meticulously the players prepare for their forthcoming round while on the practice range. The following four pages demonstrate the best ways to practise before a competition round.

Pre-round practice routine

Begin by removing all clubs from your bag and laying them out in ascending order on the ground. Starting with your lob or sand wedge, work through your lineup of clubs hitting three or four shots with each. Now hit five shots with your driver, as you will probably need to use this regularly on the course. When you have finished this process, go back and hit a few more shots with any particular club that you did not feel comfortable with. To finish, hit a series of wedge shots to your ideal lay-up yardage. This helps you feel comfortable hitting wedges from 90 metres (100 yards), which is a key area that will have a huge bearing on your momentum when you reach the course.

Half wedge shots

One of the hardest shots that you can face on the course is the half wedge shot. Making a soft, compact swing and a crisp strike to find the perfect distance requires nerves of steel. As you are more than likely to face this tricky scenario at some stage during your round, it is worth preparing for it while practising on the range.

Hit five or six shots to a target that lies around 45 metres (50 yards) away. As the pressure is off you should find a clean strike easier to achieve. This simple drill helps you set a positive mind-set for a tricky shot once you are on the course.

Sensible practice

Make sure that you do not speed through this process too quickly and resist the temptation of hitting too many shots. It is important to arrive on the first tee fresh. If you rush through this routine, playing innumerable shots, you may lack sufficient energy by the end of your competition round.

Short-game drill

A comprehensive, short-game practice routine is also an important part of your pre-round preparations. Your aim here should simply be to develop a feel for the pace of the greens and the density of the grass surrounding them. Hit a series of long and short putts and chips so that you are prepared for how your ball will react to the greens.

Hold your finish

Many amateurs hit one ball on the range after the other, without taking the care to see where they end up but watching each shot helps you gain a feel for how the ball is travelling and how conditions are affecting its flight. Hold your finish position until the ball lands, because this also promotes a rhythmical, balanced swing.

Playing the course on the range

An alternative method of preparing yourself for the round ahead is to play the course while on the range. This process involves visualizing each hole and the shots you face while honing your skills for the specific challenges that you are about to take on. Here is all you need to know about how to play the course while on the range.

Long game

After a short warm-up session (hitting a few wedges and a couple of longer shots), picture yourself standing on the first tee. Imagine the hole stretched out in front of you and take out the club that you intend to play. Hit the ball and visualize exactly where it would finish on that hole. Play a second shot from where you expect the first to have finished. If you would be hitting a punch with a 7-iron, then that is the shot you should play here. Alternatively, if you would be chipping out of the trees, then do so. Work through all 18 holes playing the sort of shots that you would expect to face on the course itself.

Chipping

If you believe your approach shot would have missed the green, hit a chip. Think about the sort of short-game escape required and the type of flight needed to get the ball close to the flag. Whether it is a flop shot or a chip-and-run, pick an appropriate target on the range as if you were playing to a pin on the course.

Shot-shaping

Playing the course while on the range works well because it acts as the perfect mental rehearsal for the round ahead. There should be no surprises in store that you are unable to cope with. If any particular tee shot or approach requires a certain shape – a draw or a fade – try to hit it.

Stand behind your ball, picture the appropriate hole and visualize the required flight. Now address the ball, taking extra care to ensure that your feet and clubface are aiming in the correct positions (see pages 58–65). If you have problems controlling the amount of sidespin that you impart on the ball, you should focus on this shot at the end of the practice session by hitting five or six shots with the specific intention of improving your control of the fade or draw.

On the course

Take on to the course the same visual rehearsal that you used on the range. As you stand over each shot, picture making a smooth swing that delivers the ideal ball flight. Imagine the ball flying perfectly towards its target. This helps you focus on a positive outcome.

Mastering the first tee

It might be frustrating to hear but you need more than just a good technique to produce consistently low scores: you need to be able to control your nerves. Fortunately, this is a skill that any player can develop. The following advice helps you overcome the tension and intimidation of the opening tee shot.

Club selection

If you are feeling nervous as you stand on the first tee, select the club that you feel most confident using. For example, choose your rescue club if you rely on it for a solid, accurate strike. The most important thing is for the ball to find the fairway and so prevent a high score from putting you at a disadvantage from the start of the round. Therefore do not be afraid to leave your driver in the bag on the first tee.

Visualization

How often do you stand over your ball, looking down at the fairway or green and your view is dominated by trees, water or deep rough? Making a committed swing is almost impossible when all you perceive is potential disaster. Create a positive outlook by standing behind your ball and imagining the ideal shot. This simple tip prevents negative thoughts from having a detrimental impact on your swing.

Swing thoughts

Try to have just one simple swing thought to improve your focus. This should be to concentrate on swinging through to a full, balanced finish position. Such a thought gives you a good chance of finding your target, and prevents any jerky movements from destroying your rhythm. Many amateurs become paralyzed by the sheer number of swing thoughts running through their minds as they prepare to hit the ball. Thinking of swing paths, wrist hinges, clubhead angles and angles of attack will only prevent you from making a smooth and committed swing.

Ready to fire

It is important to prevent nervous tension from building up. Once you are happy that you have set a good address position, start your backswing. If you freeze over the ball, tension will start to build up.

Key points for pre-round preparations

- Use your practice round to gain a feel for the specific type of layout you will face, and develop the shots that you will need to play it.

- Warm up your upper and lower body to improve flexibility and avoid injury.

- Hit shots on the range before moving to the course. Either run through your bag hitting a couple of shots with each club or imagine that you are playing each hole.

- On the first tee use a club that you feel comfortable with and swing through to a full, balanced finish.

TROUBLESHOOTING

The line between emphatic success and infuriating failure can be excruciatingly fine. One small wrong movement can leave your scorecard in tatters. The worst part is that it is often difficult to tell the difference between a good swing that sends the ball soaring arrow-straight towards its target and a bad one that embarrasses and frustrates in equal measures. This chapter helps you solve the most devastating problems. It starts with the most frequent faults of all – slicing and hooking.

Slicing

As the club cuts across the ball through impact it imparts left-to-right spin, which causes the destructive slicing flight. Perhaps the most common reason behind this fault is an exaggerated, out-to-in swing path.

Cure: headcover drill

1 To prevent this movement, place the headcover of your driver on the ground, to the right and slightly behind your ball, as shown. If the swing path is your problem, you will strike the headcover before you make contact with the ball.

2 To hone a more reliable, in-to-out swing path, concentrate on missing the headcover obstacle. This forces you to attack the ball from inside the ball-to-target line.

Takeaway problems

The path of your swing shapes the ball flight so pay attention to the route the club takes on the way back. If you can move the club along the correct path at the start of the swing and make a long, sweeping takeaway (see pages 30–31), your accuracy should improve, leading to a more effective angle of attack and straighter shots.

Grip problems

Without realizing it, your hold of a club can change, causing wayward shots. The good news is that the solution is relatively simple if this is your problem.

Cure: check your grip

To check that your grip has not moved to become either too weak (causing a slice) or too strong (causing a hook), place your hands on the club and look at where the 'v' between the thumb and forefinger of your right hand points. If your grip is to blame for your slice it will point towards your chin. If you are suffering with a hook it will aim to the right of your right shoulder. Ideally, the 'v' between your thumb and forefinger should point towards your right shoulder, as shown.

If you need to adjust your grip, allow for an awkward transition period. Spend time on the range becoming accustomed to your new hold before playing for real; if you do not, you will get frustrated and you will be more likely to revert to your bad habits.

Hooking

If you hook the ball by sending it low to the left with right-to-left spin, you need to work on the synchronization of your arms and body. If your arms are working ahead of your body you will naturally close the clubface through impact.

Cure: better synchronization

Make a series of practice swings with just one hand on the club, ensuring that your right elbow moves in perfect harmony with your right hip. Also concentrate on preventing your right hand from releasing too soon through the impact area. After a series of one-handed practice swings, hit a ball for real. Your hands and body should work together, preventing the clubface from closing.

Pushing and pulling

Pushing and pulling are two frustrating faults caused by the clubface pointing straight right or left of the target – not by sidespin generated at impact. The good news is that solving this problem should be relatively simple. The following advice is designed to help you repair the damage when these ugly shots appear while on the course.

Alignment check

If you are suffering with a push or pull, the first thing to check is your alignment. Ensure that your clubface is aiming directly at the target and that your feet, hips and shoulders are all perfectly square to your ball-to-target line. If any one of these components is off line, you risk pushing or pulling the shot.

If you are suffering with a pull, set up to the shot holding the club in your right hand, then build your stance from here. This will ensure that at address your shoulders are not closed – the most common reason behind a pull.

If you are struggling to tame your push, hold the club in your left hand when doing your alignment check.

Push fix

Leaving the clubface open through impact and pushing the ball to the right is a sure sign of a hesitant swing. If you are nervous, it can be difficult to commit to a shot and release the clubhead powerfully through the ball as you should. To solve this problem, concentrate on making an athletic body turn.

Make sure that you continue to rotate your upper body after you have struck the ball, so that your chest is at 90 degrees to your target in the finish position. This simple swing thought promotes a good release of the clubhead through impact, preventing you from leaving the face open as you strike the ball.

Pull fix

Many amateurs have an in-built fear of hitting the ball to the right. If you are used to seeing your ball veer off in that direction, it is hard not to aim left as a safeguard. But if the clubface points left and then returns square through impact, a pull is the probable result.

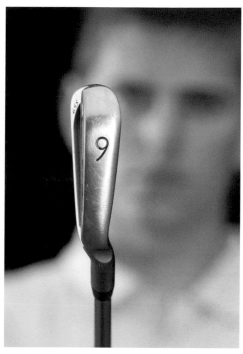

1 Stand behind the ball and pick your target, using the line of your shaft to aim. This should prevent you from aiming left.

2 Having set up square to the target, make sure that the face is exactly perpendicular to the ground. This ensures that the clubface is not closed at address.

Jargon buster

'Pulled' Your ball is said to be pulled when it flies on a straight line but left of your target.

'Pushed' Your ball is said to be pushed when it flies arrow-straight but to the right of your target.

Fatting and thinning

Imagine this scenario: you are standing on the middle of the fairway with a straightforward, 137-metre (150-yard) approach to the green. You have a realistic prospect of making a birdie, yet you make a terrible contact. Fatting and thinning are two common faults that will turn a good situation bad within the blink of an eye. If these faults appear regularly, it will be impossible to complete a round with a respectable score still intact. Here are their causes and how you can solve them.

Poor posture

Fatting and thinning are two very different shots but the reasons for their ugly appearance are similar. One of the main causes is losing your height during the swing. If your head rises or dips before you have struck the ball, the bottom of your swing arc will be either too low or too high, and fat or thin contacts are the most likely outcome.

You can prevent this destructive vertical head movement by making some practice swings without a club, with your head resting against a wall. Take your address position and place a towel between your forehead and the wall. Now make a series of practice swings. If your head rises or dips, the towel will fall down.

Stiff right knee

If you are suffering from fat or thin strikes while on the course, concentrate on the flex in your right knee during the swing. Many amateurs make the mistake of standing up as they reach the top of the backswing, losing the bend in the right knee.

By concentrating on maintaining the flex in your right knee while you play your shot, you should be able to retain the athletic posture that you set at address, thereby increasing your chances of a better contact.

Incorrect weight distribution

The reverse pivot is a common mistake caused by moving your weight in the wrong direction during the swing (see pages 56–57). As you hang back on your right side through the downswing, the bottom of the swing arc will come before you make contact with the ball. This means that fat and thin contact will be a regular occurrence.

Solve this problem by placing a towel under your right foot before hitting a series of practice shots. This simple drill forces your weight on to your left side.

As you drive your arms through the downswing you should feel your weight moving in the same direction as your arms – towards the target.

Curing the shank

If slicing is the game's most common fault, then shanking is by far the most destructive. As your ball shoots off on a 45-degree angle towards the rough, trees or water, your scorecard will record the disappointment. It is often said that a shank is desperately close to the perfect shot, but that is scant consolation when your ball becomes buried in the undergrowth. Follow these tips to stamp out this painful problem.

Leaning in

When the club returns to the ball farther to the right than it was at address, you hit a shank. This can be caused by your body swaying towards the ball fractionally through the downswing. Although leaning in is only a small fault, it will take some dedicated work to eradicate it from your muscle memory.

Cure: balls-under-toes drill

To force your weight away from the ends of your toes and more towards your heels, place a ball under the toes of each foot, as shown. This prevents you from leaning in, either at set-up or through the downswing, and striking the ball from the hosel.

Cure: tennis ball drill

To help you stop striking the ball too far out of the heel, place two tennis balls on the ground either side of your ball, as shown. Hit a series of practice shots aiming to hit the golf ball without making contact with the tennis balls. Here, the tennis balls acts as an excellent visual aid, which should help you find the middle of the clubface more consistently.

Incorrect weight movements

If your weight moves towards the ball through the downswing, a shank is the likely outcome.

Cure: practice on one foot

To highlight whether this is a problem for you hit some shots while standing on one foot. By destabilizing the base of your swing, you will get an acute feel for how your weight moves. If you are leaning into the ball through impact, you will be forced to take a step to the right to steady yourself. Practice hitting shots on one foot until you can hold the finish position without taking a step.

Wayward swing

It is difficult for some players to detect why they shank the ball. In this situation, the reason can be simply that you are throwing your arms away from your body fractionally through the downswing. As your arms move too far from your body, a heel strike is the probable result.

Cure: scorecard-under-arm drill

To prevent such a destructive movement, place a scorecard under your arm and hit some practice shots. If you are indeed throwing your arms away from your body, the card will fall to the ground during your downswing.

Destabilize your swing to discover whether you are leaning in to the ball.

Use your scorecard to help your arms stay close to your body.

Jargon buster

'Hosel' The point above the heel where the shaft joins the clubhead.

'Shanking' Refers to when the ball strikes the junction between the shaft and the clubface, causing it to shoot off at a 45-degree angle.

Checking your fundamentals

The majority of long game faults can be traced back to problems at address. Your set-up position therefore should be the first thing to check whenever you are struggling with your game. Here are four quick and easy ways to help you establish the key positions for more consistent, accurate golf.

Posture

By far the best and easiest way to check your posture is to look at your reflection in the mirror. When doing this there are three key things to look out for. Make sure that your back is straight and that your shoulders are not hunched over the ball. Check that there is a reasonable amount of flex in your legs. Take a look at the angle of your arms. Ideally they should hang vertically down as your upper body bends over the ball. This will create about a hands width of space between the top of your thigh and the butt end of the club.

Swing path

While standing at the mirror to check your posture you can also look at your swing path. Take the club back and stop halfway through the backswing, as shown.

In the perfect position, the club should dissect your shoulder and the butt end of the shaft should be pointing at the ball. If you find it impossible to reach this position automatically, you could be swinging the club along a destructive path that will cost you accuracy.

Accuracy check

A simple way to check your alignment
and ball position is a technique used by
many of the best golfers as they practise
on ranges around the world. At the start
of any practice routine lay a shaft on the
ground parallel to your ball-to-target
line. This will act as a handy reference to
how accurately your body and clubface
are aligned throughout. Make sure that
your feet, hips and shoulders are all
parallel to your ball-to-target line and
pay close attention to your ball position
(see pages 18–19). These checks are
guaranteed to help improve not only
your alignment but also your swing path.

Poor grip

A good grip has a huge bearing on
whether you can return the clubface
square to the target through impact so it
is essential to check this regularly. You
can do this easily by taking your normal
grip and extending the forefinger of your
right hand. In the ideal position this
finger should point at your left foot. If it
is directed towards your right foot, you
have a weak grip, which means you are
far more likely to slice the ball. If your
finger points outside your left foot, you
have likely to play some destructive
hooks. To correct a slice or hook see
pages 96–97.

Controlling your wedge play

One of the major areas where professionals show their expertise and amateurs are often left disappointed is when playing from inside 110 metres (120 yards). With a wedge in hand, the world's best players are thinking about hitting their ball to within 3 metres (10 ft) of the flag. The reason for their confidence is that, through dedicated practice, they have developed an innate feeling for the type of shot required. The following guide and some hard work of your own will help you find the target when you reach your scoring zone.

Dirty grooves

To control the distance of your wedges, it helps to impart a good amount of backspin on the ball at impact so that it stops quickly when it hits the green. A crisp contact is a prerequisite to producing backspin, but the grooves of your wedge will also need to be clean. If there is mud or wet grass on the face, the grooves will be unable to grip the ball through impact and to impart backspin. So after you make your practice swing, and before you hit the ball for real, always wipe or better still brush the face of your wedge clean.

Key points for troubleshooting

- When struggling with a hook or slice, check your grip and make sure the clubhead moves from inside to outside the ball-to-target line through impact.

- Prevent pushing and pulling the ball by taking extra care over the alignment of your body and clubface at address.

- Stop fatting and thinning the ball by driving your weight towards the target through the downswing.

- Make sure that your weight is not moving into the ball through the downswing to avoid shanking.

- Alter the length of your back- and through-swing to find different, awkward yardages with your wedges.

Poor swing control

You need to make subtle differences in the strength of your swing to reach different distances; you need to hit the ball softer at a flag 55 metres (60 yards) away than at one 110 metres (120 yards) away, but delivering a crisp contact that finds the right length is tricky. Picture a clockface to help improve your control.

1 On the practice range hit ten shots by swinging your hands to nine o'clock on the backswing to three o'clock on the throughswing. Concentrate on this movement over each shot. Now mark down on a piece of paper the average distance you achieved. This is the perfect length for your nine o'clock swing.

2 Hit ten balls by swinging to ten o'clock with your hands on the way back and two o'clock on the way through. Focus on maintaining the rhythm of your swing (it is easy to speed up here). A longer swing will translate to longer shots, so mark down the average distance for your ten o'clock swing.

3 Hit ten shots by swinging to 11 o'clock with your hands on the way back and one o'clock on the way through. Mark down the average length for your 11 o'clock swing. Memorize these figures as they will be crucial in helping you find the right swing to control the distance of your wedges when you reach the course.

MIND GAMES AND TACTICS

Performing well under pressure is what separates an average score from an excellent one. This requires a sound strategy that allows you to play to your strengths and the mental fortitude to block out potentially destructive negative thoughts. This chapter helps you cope with the mental strain of 18 competitive holes, whether by devising a clever game plan or by showing you how to hold on to your nerve when you most need to do so.

Strategic success

Every player sees the same golf course in a slightly different way. If you favour a right-to-left, drawing ball flight there will be some holes that fit your natural shape, while others do not. Whenever a particular hole does not suit your style, you may have to adjust your usual strategy for a safe result, and a course planner will help you do this. It should provide you with a definitive guide for which club to use in any situation, as it gives yardages to each of the major dangers on any particular hole. It will help you decide when to attack and when to defend. Use a club that takes the major hazards out of play on any tough hole and attack whenever you feel the odds are stacked in your favour and the penalty for a bad shot is not so severe.

Use the stroke index

The stroke index is a guide printed on your scorecard and on plaques on every tee, which ranks each hole from one to 18 in terms of difficulty (one is the hardest, 18 is the easiest). Many players struggle when playing the low-numbered holes on the stroke index, so as long as you do not record a high number you are unlikely to lose ground on the field. When playing such difficult holes, use a strategy that helps you keep your score intact. Even if it means playing with an iron off the tee for safety, your main priority should be to keep your momentum moving forwards. When the stroke index of a particular hole is high, you can attack, in the knowledge that this is one of the easier holes you face. By using the stroke index you can manage your expectations effectively while on the course in order to record the best possible score.

When facing a tough lie

Amateur golfers are often guilty of making poor decisions, exaggerating already bad mistakes. If you have missed the fairway and face a tough lie, just try to get your ball back on the cut grass.

Take a wedge and swing aggressively through the grass to a safe part of the fairway. This tactic will help you avoid the sort of high scores that are guilty of destroying many players' cards.

Coping with pressure

To play well when it matters the most you will need to take control of your emotions. Preventing nervous tension from causing a jerky swing and remaining focused and calm at all times are so important that the majority of top players work towards this end with a sports psychologist. Your mind can be your most powerful tool but only if you know how to use it...

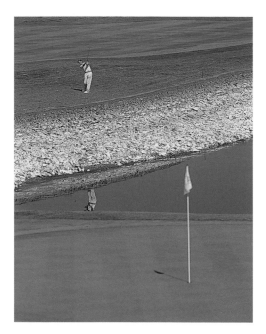

Playing over water

The prospect of hitting your ball over a lake is an intimidating one that requires a positive, committed swing. In this situation, you must attack with conviction or else risk producing a nervous, tentative swing. It might sound strange but it is a good idea to play with one less club than usual in this situation. This tactic forces you into making an aggressive swing and the faster clubhead speed through impact means that you should still make it over the water, even if the quality of the strike is not perfect.

Picking your target

An excellent technique that helps you improve your accuracy is to aim at as small a target as possible. Pick a distinctive feature on the horizon - such as a building, the top of a tree or a utility post - and picture an imaginary line between this spot and your ball. Then as you set up for the shot, pick a mark on this line just in front of your ball.

As you prepare to strike the shot, aim to hit your ball over this mark. By narrowing your aim as much as possible your accuracy is guaranteed to improve.

Pre-shot routine

There are certain techniques that you can use to help you feel comfortable and confident while competing. The most common of these is to have a pre-shot routine, that is to undertake a series of actions that allows you to focus positively on the shot in hand and prepare for a fluid swing. By running through the following actions before hitting the ball, you will enter a comfort zone – a type of auto-pilot that helps you focus on a positive result. If you run through the same set of actions before every long-game shot, you should start to feel far more comfortable under pressure.

1 After teeing up your ball, stand back and look at the hole ahead. Visualize the ideal shot, how you expect the ball to shape through the air and where you want it to land. Make a couple of practice swings, rehearsing for the sort of swing that you are looking to deliver.

2 Just before addressing the ball, relax yourself by taking three deep breaths (see pages 46–47). Now take your stance, ensuring that your body and clubface are perfectly aligned (see pages 16–17). Breathe out through the downswing.

Matchplay masterclass

One of the reasons that the Ryder Cup is golf's most treasured event is that the world's best are pitted against each other and are fighting hard for a prize made of pride and not money. In a matchplay competition, each player is involved in a head-to-head battle against another player, and to succeed requires tactics that will deflect pressure from you on to your opponent.

Finding the fairway

Never take any risks from the tee unless you are down in your match and are desperate to make a move. Finding the fairway can be crucial in stroke play, and its importance is doubled in matchplay. If you make a poor tee shot, you automatically hand the initiative for that hole to your opponent, but when you find your target the pressure of matching your good shot is intensified for him or her. If you can cut your mistakes down to the bare minimum you should fair well.

Pressurizing your opponent

There are certain tactics that you can use to unsettle your opponent. For example, if you are longer than him or her off the tee, walk up and stand next to your ball as he plays his second shot (but make sure that you are nowhere near his line of fire). Your sheer presence ahead of him on the fairway, bearing down on the green, will make him feel slightly uneasy and might just provoke a nervous swing.

Controlling your emotions

Your emotions will expose your mental state for all to see, so when competing in matchplay it is important not to give your opponent the sense that you are rattled or feeling under pressure. Never react badly to a poor shot. Even if you have missed the green and landed in a difficult area, do not air your frustration as this will galvanize the opposition. Instead, take it calmly. This will give the impression that you have got the skills to get out of trouble.

Jargon buster

'Fourball' In a foursome round in a competition (either in strokeplay or matchplay), four golfers each play their own ball during the round. Usually the four golfers are split into two teams of two. The best score from either player in each team counts towards the final total.

'Foursome' In a foursome round in a competition (either in strokeplay or matchplay), two teams of two play alongside each other. Each team plays one ball, which the players hit alternately.

Team matchplay

When playing alongside a partner in a fourball or foursome, your job should be to take the pressure off your teammate as much as possible. When you are on the green, make sure that you do not leave him with too many tricky 1.5-metre (5-ft) putts. It is also important to demonstrate solidarity with your partner. Show your opponents that you are a strong team, working together, and they are guaranteed to find this somewhat intimidating.

Building a medal score

If you are embarking on a competitive-medal round, prepare yourself for an emotional rollercoaster. Your desperation to score well will create serious internal pressure. The strength of your game plan can either accentuate or alleviate this tension. Here is how to make a series of sensible choices.

Approach play

The flag provides an obvious target to aim at when approaching the green, yet on the majority of occasions in matchplay the hole is cut in one corner of the green. In such a case you should aim at the middle of the green. As long as your club selection is correct you should end up with a reasonable birdie chance.

Attacking a tight pin is risky. If you are slightly out, you will face a delicate chip from an inevitably tough lie. By taking the pin out of your mind-set, your margin for error will greatly increase.

Check your distances

How long do you spend deciding which club to use? Many amateurs pay close attention to the line without taking enough care over the distance, and the most common mistake here is to under-club. It is always very important to check your distances. Most courses have 137-metre (150-yard) markers on the fairways to help you select the right club. If you use these guides, you will not have to rely on your instincts. You should also consider the strength and direction of the wind, drawing a picture in your mind of the ideal ball flight, before deciding which club to play with.

Swing thought

Many of the best players in the world are so instinctive about their technique that they do not think of anything in particular as they prepare to take the club back. A clear mind enables them to make a fluid swing. But if you are less sure about the mechanics of your movement you may wish to concentrate on avoiding your most common mistakes. A good way to do this is to use one simple thought to help you make a solid swing – whether it is a long, wide takeaway or full, balanced finish position. Make sure that you have just one trigger thought for a positive effect. If you have any more than that, you risk the sort of confusion that leads to a rigid and unnatural movement.

Avoiding disaster

The majority of bad scores are caused by just one or two disastrous holes. Whenever you have made a mistake by missing the fairway or green, your primary concern should be to give yourself a chance of salvaging a respectable score. Get the ball back into play as soon as possible, and you will avoid turning a simple mistake into a disaster.

Jargon buster

'Yardage markers' Coloured posts or plates on the fairway or in the rough, marking points usually 137 metres (150 yards) and 90 metres (100 yards) away from the green.

Finishing a good score

How many times have you reached the 15th tee with a good score beckoning only to blow it with a disastrous finish? This is one of the most demoralising experiences a golfer can have, and it leaves a bad taste that lingers long in the mouth. Once you have thrown away a good score you will try anything to avoid doing it again – here is how to do it effectively.

Swinging with conviction

One of the most common mistakes made over the final few holes is to try and steer your ball towards the target in search of greater control. But this can actually lead to an unnatural movement and a wayward shot. One simple swing thought can help you commit to a good strike, and so avoid this problem. Concentrate on driving your weight on to your left side through impact, so that your right heel lifts off the ground in the finish position, as shown (below right). Such a movement means you are far more likely to make a sweet, powerful strike, and it helps you avoid a flat-footed swing.

Trying to steer your ball towards the target can result in a flat-footed swing and missing your target.

If your weight is on your left side through impact, you should finish with your right heel off the ground.

Stay in the present

The old cliché about not getting ahead of yourself when you are achieving a decent score is crucial here. If your attention drifts to a tough shot later in the round, you risk making a simple mistake before you get there. Giving this scenario too much importance builds tension, therefore concentrate on the current hole, and take on the challenges of the round only as they occur.

'Go to' shot

Many of the best players have a particular shot that they can rely on under pressure. If your natural ball flight is a gentle fade, do not try and hit a draw when you are completing a good round. By overcomplicating matters while under pressure you can turn a straightforward shot into a difficult one. If you make a mistake you will be left to rue this decision.

Key points for tactics

- Before a round, devise a game plan that helps you play to your strengths.

- Employ a simple and repeatable pre-shot routine and control your breathing to alleviate nervous tension.

- When taking on another player in a matchplay format, your priority should always be to keep the ball in play.

- Aim for the middle of the green and not necessarily at the flag to give yourself a greater margin for error.

- Have one simple swing thought to help you commit to a solid swing, and concentrate on the current hole, and not on one that you will reach later in the round.

M●VING FORWARD

Having worked your way through this book to the final chapter you should now have a solid understanding of the mechanic of the golf swing – from stance and posture to swing path and weight distribution. There is a lot to take in. Genuine success requires devotion to an effective practice plan to ensure that all of these important facets are in place. This chapter shows you how to take your game to the next level.

Consult your pro

To make a lasting improvement to your swing it is important to take regular lessons with a qualified professional. He will be able to assess the areas that need attention, and he can provide you with tips, drills and swing thoughts to get you moving in the right way. Ultimately, if your technique improves you are more likely to shoot lower scores, so it is usually well worth the investment in both time and money. And if you have regular lessons over a period of months or years, the professional will get to know your strengths and weaknesses, and his detached, impartial eye will help you whenever you require some guidance.

Take notes

Many amateurs fail to analyse their score after a competitive round but they should, because this helps you identify the specific areas of your game that need improvement. After you play note down on your scorecard the number of fairways you have hit, the number of greens you have found and the number of putts you have taken. Then keep the card for reference. Over a period of weeks and months you will be able to identify what areas of your game you need to concentrate on in practice.

Learn from the best

You will be pleased to hear that one of the most effective ways to improve is simply by watching the top players in the world on television. By scrutinizing the technique of Tiger Woods, Ernie Els or Retief Goosen, for example, you will see how a solid swing should look. They all have a perfect posture, and they remain well balanced throughout the swing. By having a picture of their technique in your mind when you swing, your own mechanics are likely to improve without having to work too hard on the range.

It is also worth watching how such top players prepare to play. The majority of them have a pre-shot routine to help focus on the situation at hand. Again, if you copy one particular pre-shot routine that you like, you are likely to become a better player.

Good and bad practice

Heading off to your local driving range and bashing balls aimlessly for an hour is much like going to the gym without a workout plan – you are in serious danger of doing more harm than good. However, if you know what you are doing practising is neither boring nor time-consuming. The following advice shows you how to train for competition.

Trigger happy

One of the most common sights at any driving range is someone hitting drive after drive in a bid to try and impress bystanders and clear the back fence. But hitting too many drives can ruin your rhythm. It is inevitable that you speed up as you go in search of that perfect tee shot. Remember to hit just a few shots with a driver at the end of your routine. This will enable you to maintain control and will prevent you from losing synchronization between your arms and body during the swing.

Slow down

When you are faced with the prospect of hitting 50 or even 100 practice balls, the tendency is often to speed through them. Make sure that you do not go reaching for the next ball as soon as you have just hit a practice shot. After each shot (good or bad), hold your finish position until the ball lands. If it was a poor shot, analyze the movement that you just made, then make a practice swing trying to feel what you should be doing instead. If you speed through your basket of balls you will find it very difficult to assess what exactly is going right and wrong.

Take notes

Whenever you practise it is always a good idea to note down what you are trying to improve and how you are doing it. This way if you start making the same mistake in the future you will be able to find the perfect cure in your notebook.

Too many balls

If you have been playing poorly it is sensible to visit the range. While there, however, make sure that you do not hit too many balls. As you start to tire you are likely to become lazy, and you might develop faults such as swinging. Think of 100 balls as your absolute maximum, and if you start to feel tired do not be too proud to leave some balls behind on the range.

Judging distances

If you know exactly how far you hit the ball, the percentage of greens that you hit in the correct number of shots will always be high. Distance control is just as important as accuracy so it makes sense to devote some time to this while on the range. The following handy tips will help you determine exactly how far you hit the ball with each club in the bag.

Make a reference

To find out how far you hit the ball make a visit to the range, do a warm-up and hit ten shots with each club in the bag.

For each club, measure how far the average ball has travelled and note this number down on the sticker on the shaft. When you get to the course and are planning your attack on any particular green you will have a reference, written on the club, for exactly how far you hit the ball.

Technical guidance

Use the opportunity when on a launch monitor being custom-fitted for a set of clubs to seek guidance from the custom-fit technician as to the specific areas of your technique that require improvement. The data provided gives a clear impression of how the ball leaves the clubface at impact. If you are hitting the ball with too much back- or sidespin the data will highlight this. If you find the results disconcerting, take them to your local pro for some advice on how to improve.

On the course

When you are on the course, it is essential that you find an exact yardage for every approach shot that you play. In addition to a course planner, there are usually yardage markers on the edge of the fairways or on sprinkler heads.

Pace out the distance from these points to your ball to help you select the right club for your next shot. One long adult stride is usually about 1 yard (1 m).

Which measurement point?

If you are using a course planner to plot your route to each green, always check in the front of the book to see whether the yardages are to the front or middle of the green. This varies a great deal and is always worth checking, because, if you get it wrong, your accuracy will be consistently out during the round.

Key points for moving forward

• Have regular lessons with a qualified professional to help you make a lasting change.

• Practise effectively by going to the range with a plan and by not hitting too many balls in one session.

• Determine exactly how far you hit each club in the bag on the practice ground. Then note down these yardage for reference when you get to the course.

FAULT-FIXER CHECKLIST

If you are experiencing a bad day on the course and you feel a good score is slipping through your fingers, you might be able to make a small but crucial change. Knowing exactly what to do might just salvage your score, so if you are experiencing a rough ride try to implement these technical tips.

Slicing
- Make sure that your grip is not too weak.
- Practise swinging the club from inside to outside the ball-to-target line through impact.
- Make a wide takeaway and concentrate on releasing your hands through impact.
- Do not aim to the left.

Hooking
- Make sure that your grip is not too strong.
- Try to ensure that your arms and body rotate at the same speed through the downswing.
- Make sure that your hands do not release too soon, that is, before impact.
- Do not aim to the right

Pushing
- Make sure that your clubface is aiming directly at the target.
- Set your body square to your ball-to-target line.
- Concentrate on completing your body turn on both the backswing and throughswing.

Pulling
- Ensure that your clubface and body are aligned to the target.
- As you address the ball use just your right hand to hold the club to prevent your shoulders from closing.
- Hold the club up at address to check where the face is pointing.

Lack of power
- Stretch your upper and lower body to improve your flexibility.
- Start your downswing by dropping your hands straight down.
- Accelerate your hands steadily through the downswing
- Waggle the club at address to relieve tension.

Fatting and thinning
- Make sure that your weight moves on to your right side during the backswing.
- Drive your weight on to your left side through impact.
- Ensure that your head does not dip or lift before you have struck the ball.

Shanking
- At address make sure that your weight is not too far forward, that is, on the ends of your toes.
- Do not move your weight towards the ball through the downswing.
- Make sure that your arms do not move too far away from your body as you attack the ball.

Struggling under pressure
- Breathe slowly and deliberately to relieve any built-up tension.
- Set a positive mental outlook by visualizing your shot before playing it.
- Concentrate on one key swing thought.
- Do not pause unnecessarily at address as tension will build up.

Poor ball striking
- Work on establishing a solid set-up position.
- Try to maintain your balance, and do not hit the ball too hard.
- Make sure that your arms and body swing in harmony through the downswing.
- Make a series of practice swings with your eyes shut.

Bad distance control
- Use yardage markers and a course planner to help you pick the perfect distance.
- Pay careful attention to the weather conditions.
- Consider where the trouble surrounding the greens lies – if it is all at the front, take one extra club.

Difficult conditions
- Widen your stance to provide extra stability.
- Move the ball back in your stance to ensure a crisp contact.
- Think smart and play within yourself; do not try to pull off a miraculous shot.
- Keep your grips dry and your studs clean.

If you have been struggling with a serious fault, pay close attention to the fundamentals at address, as well as the key swing mechanics.

Index

Acknowledgments

The author and publisher would like to thank West Kent Golf Club for their generosity and hospitality during the photoshoot and also Chris Forsyth, Mike Evans, Katie Dawkins and Nick Korynevsky for taking part.

Executive Editor Trevor Davies
Editor Lisa John
Executive Art Editor Darren Southern
Designer Peter Gerrish
Illustrations Sudden Impact Media
Senior Production Controller Martin Croshaw
Picture Librarian Sophie Delpech

Special Photography © Octopus Publishing Group Limited/Angus Murray.

Other photography:
Alamy/Popperfoto 63 right.
Corbis UK Ltd/Steven Georges 74.
Getty Images/Harry How 119 right.
Octopus Publishing Group Limited/Nick Walker 110 left.
Proshot Solutions/www.proshotsolutions.co.uk 13 bottom, 122 right.